# H₂O architecture

# H$_2$O architecture

stephen crafti

images
Publishing

Reprinted in 2005
The Images Publishing Group Reference Number: 638

Published in Australia in 2005 by
The Images Publishing Group Pty Ltd
ABN 89 059 734 431
6 Bastow Place, Mulgrave, Victoria, 3170, Australia
Telephone: +61 3 9561 5544  Facsimilie: +61 3 9561 4860
Email: books@images.com.au
Website: www.imagespublishing.com

National Library of Australia
Cataloguing-in-Publication entry:
Crafti, Stephen, 1959–.


H20 architecture.

Includes index.

ISBN 1 86470 114 5.


1. Architecture, Domestic.
2. Water and architecture.
3. Water in landscape architecture.  I. Title.

720.47

Designed by The Graphic Image Studio Pty Ltd, Mulgrave, Australia
Website: www.tgis.com.au


Film by SC (Sang Choy) International Pte Ltd
Printed by Everbest Printing Co. Ltd, in Hong Kong/China


IMAGES has included on its website a page for special notices in relation to this and its other publications.
Please visit: www.imagespublishing.com

# contents

# introduction

Water has always been an integral feature of domestic interiors, whether it takes the shape of a luxurious built-in pool and cabana, or a rudimentary structure above ground. The sound of splashing water is firmly in our psyche. Memories of Mum calling from the house, 'I think you've had enough now', are as clear as the sky-blue tiles that lined many of these swimming pools during the 1970s. Three decades later, the colour of the tiles has changed, and water may appear on the edge of the living room, at the entrance or even within the home itself.

The water featured in this book is cleverly incorporated into the home environment. In one design, a lap pool slices two pavilions, creating a dynamic vista for both. Other pools of water frame the entrance and take the form of a pond or channel of water leading to the front door and continuing to the interior space. The water not only provides a guide to exploring the home, but also adds a calming resonance to the interior, in addition to the exterior spaces.

Some architects prefer to fill their homes with water. In one instance, a house has an indoor pool, complete with wet edges. The divisions between the hard and watery surfaces are deliberately blurred. Other architects use water to define spaces within the home. Instead of a wall between the lounge and dining area, a shallow canal divides the two spaces. The sound of water creates tranquillity in both areas.

Other architects include swimming pools – increasingly lap pools, on the edge of the living spaces. With increased knowledge about the harmful effects of the sun, providing large unprotected bodies of water at a distance from the home is diminishing. Instead, protected lap pools on the edge of the home are cleverly incorporated into the architecture. And in some cases, the water flows under a balcony and enters into the living space itself.

Creating pools that can be used all year round is also becoming more attractive. Whether a lap pool is protected by the edge of the house or apartment, or a completely enclosed swimming pool, the idea is to have a body of water that can be used regardless of weather conditions.

While many bodies of water are used for recreational purposes, other water elements create unique interior design. Fishponds or water features can be found at the entrance to a home. Past the front door, there may be another channel of water that directs the eye to an even larger pool of water in the back garden. Water not only muffles unwanted sound, but also brings to the interior spaces a magical reflected sunlight that plays on ceilings and walls.

The homes in this book are diverse. There are apartments and townhouses, small terraces and large homes. While the architectural styles of these homes vary, they are all enhanced by water. Whether it's the sight of water disappearing over the edge of a cliff, or the sight of arms doing freestyle in a lap pool on the edge of the dining room, the impact is memorable.

The projects featured in this book not only feature varying bodies of water in both interior and exterior spaces, but also demonstrate how water can be integrated with the architecture. Water isn't seen as an afterthought. It has been thoughtfully considered from the outset to achieve a certain goal. This book doesn't simply suggest using water for the sake of creating a 'splash', or as a means of impressing visitors. The purpose of this book is to show how, with the right imagination and skill, water can strengthen the architectural forms, making the experience of living in these homes that much richer. Even those people fortunate enough to have water views encounter a different experience with man made bodies of water surrounding them. And while the large expanses of water around many of these houses are certainly impressive, it is often the small surprising additions of water that create a home.

**From left to right:** The sound of water, Architects Ink, photography by Trevor Fox; Water illusions, Coy & Yiontis Architects, photography by Peter Clarke; An oasis in the city, Bates Smart and HPA Pty Ltd, photography by Martin Saunders and Greg Hocking; Sculpted water feature, Aludean, photography by Peter Clarke; Behind a garden wall, John Wardle Architects, photography by Trevor Mein; Lap pool within cube cluster, Alex Popov Architects, photography by Kraig Carlstrom.

# AT THE ENTRANCE

BUD BRANNIGAN ARCHITECT

This small site on the edge of the city once contained a worker's cottage. Designed by architect Bud Brannigan, the only remnants of the previous house are the foundations. The owners gained in floor area, (increasing in size from 80 to 120 square metres), and now can enjoy the front garden, which functions as another room.

The high front fence and gate act as the doorway to this home, which is accessed via a laneway. 'We wanted to make the most of the 250-square-metre site,' says Brannigan. Immediately behind the front fence is an 8- by 2-metre lap pool. On one side of the pool is a rendered concrete block boundary fence and on the other side is a narrow 0.5-metre concrete terrace, running along the edge. A toughened glass fence divides the pool from the lawn area.

The pool acts like a red carpet, welcoming guests to the home. Through the glazed front doors at the entrance to the home, is the kitchen and living area, together with a guest bedroom. The main bedroom, ensuite facilities and an open study area are located upstairs, looking into the void below. While there are glimpses of the lap pool from the living area, the best vantage point is on the front deck.

For Brannigan, the idea of the pool wasn't just to create a water feature in the front garden. It had to be used. And while the pool receives ample sunlight during the day, it's also solar heated. Water from the pool is channelled to hoses on the roof of the house, where it is heated with the sun's rays. The water is then returned to the pool.

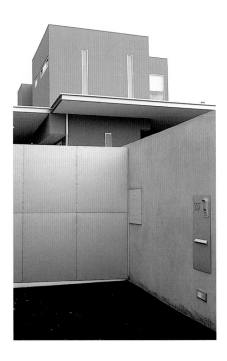

PHOTOGRAPHY BY DAVID SANDISON

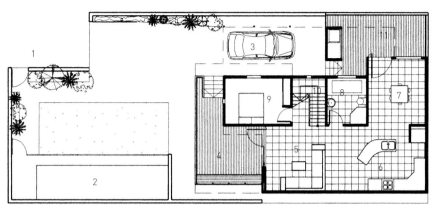

**LOWER FLOOR**

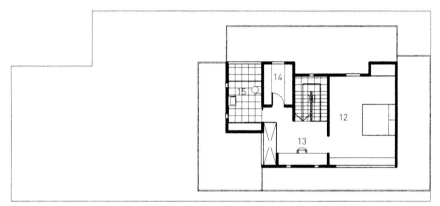

**UPPER FLOOR**

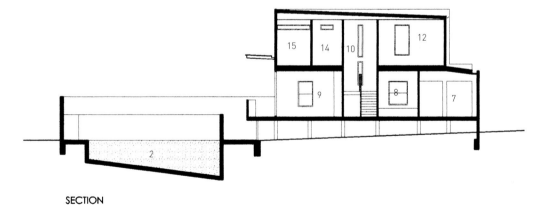

**SECTION**

1   Entry gate
2   Pool
3   Carport
4   Verandah
5   Living
6   Kitchen
7   Dining
8   Bathroom
9   Bedroom 2
10  Stairwell
11  Verandah 2
12  Bedroom 1
13  Study/work area
14  Walk in robe
15  Ensuite

# AT THE HARBOUR'S EDGE

## MARTIN PICKRELL DESIGN

This three-level house is located on the harbour's edge, as well as on the edge of a native reserve. Faced with a relatively small site of approximately 540 square metres, Pickrell appears to have carved this substantial home into the rock face.

'This house was designed to meet the requirements of a business couple wanting a town house with an emphasis on entertaining and few of the requirements of a traditional home,' says Pickrell. The building, which is accessed by a lift, features a master bedroom and garage at street level. The mid-level contains the guest apartment and the third level is dedicated to the living and entertainment area. This opens to a large pool and an additional entertainment space, with the floor below the main bedroom acting as the canopy.

The pool, approximately 15 metres in length, appears to run directly into the harbour. However, the pool has a wet edge and small Perspex lip that prevents water from splashing over the sides and down the rock face. 'On perfect days, the colour of the water from the pool and harbour read as one body of water. On any night, the pool appears to be part of the harbour,' says Pickrell.

Floor-to-ceiling glass doors in the living area further blur the division between the interior and exterior spaces. A dining room table is often placed adjacent to the pool area during the warmer months. 'This house is about the relationship to water, even if my clients don't go to the beach every day,' says Pickrell.

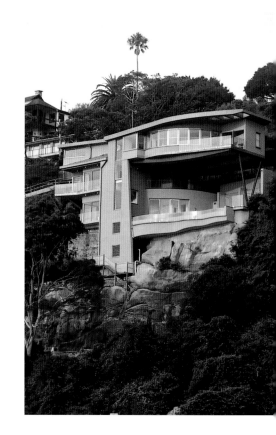

# BEHIND A GARDEN WALL

## JOHN WARDLE ARCHITECTS

When a grand Victorian-style home became too large for the owners, they decided to subdivide the site, sell the home and build a new house in their back garden. Rather than dividing the site with a linear paling fence, the architect created a curved brick wall. 'The idea of a circular garden wall seemed appropriate. This geometry is quite common in Victorian gardens,' says architect John Wardle, who was commissioned to design the new house.

Directly behind the new rendered brick wall is a 20-metre pool. Wrapping around the wall, the water appears to extend endlessly. As the pool was integral to the brief, Wardle designed the new house around it. The kitchen, dining and living areas on the ground floor have views to the pool, as do the main bedroom and ensuite. Floor-to-ceiling glass windows in the living area provide expansive views of the water. And in the dining area, a slot window at ground level offers another view. There is also direct access from the ensuite to the pool. 'The ensuite is a hybrid between a bathroom and a cabana. The owners can get up in the morning and dive straight into the pool,' says Wardle.

The two-storey house, made of zinc, rendered brickwork and timber, also features a cellar directly below the living area with a porthole window looking out to the water.

Water often features in Wardle's designs. 'Water changes from day to night. At night, it's like a massive light-box. It illuminates the entire house and environment. There's also the wonderful texture every time there's a splash,' he adds.

PHOTOGRAPHY BY TREVOR MEIN

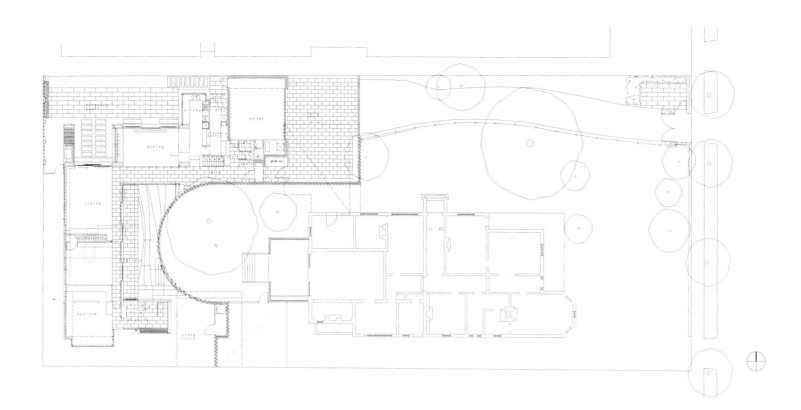

# THE CALM AND THE TURBULENT

JMA ARCHITECTS

This monumental U-shaped home was designed by architect John Mainwaring. 'It's as though it's perched on the headlands, with water crashing against the crevice,' says Mainwaring, describing the house as being strategically positioned between the pool at the front and the ocean to the rear of the site. 'Normally the pool is located on the ocean side. But we wanted to engage with the urban environment. It's also more protected away from the ocean,' he adds.

The transition between the calm and the turbulent unfolds when water changes from the stillness of a pool at the front of the house, to the roaring ocean behind. 'There's a strong energy between the two water sources which varies in strength depending on where you are in the house,' says Mainwaring. Multi-storey apartments overlook the property from the street. Their collage of pastel-rendered walls and balconies might suggest serious planting. However, instead of creating a tropical forest to eliminate the view, Mainwaring has brought the apartment colours into the site. The colour-blocked wall that defines the pool also acts as a walkway across the bridge to the front door. 'The sand and charcoal colours are also reminiscent of the nearby headlands,' he adds.

The 30-metre pool extends out at the front of the property, 1.5 metres wide at its narrowest point, and 5 metres at its broadest. 'The idea wasn't just to create a lap pool, but a substantial body of water that engaged with the urban fabric,' says Mainwaring. The main kitchen in the house was designed with easy access to the pool. However, mindful of the climate and the owners' penchant for outdoor dining, a second more informal kitchen was created adjacent to the pool. Protected by a steel, timber and polycarbonate canopy, the owners can entertain here for a substantial part of the year.

Various aspects of the home ensure that both the ocean and the pool can be appreciated. While floor-to-ceiling glazed walls and doors take in the ocean views, fenestrations created along the side elevations of the home allow a glimpse of both bodies of water. The pool is also visible from the main bedroom.

Around the pool area there are generous plantings of the local native, pandanus. As Mainwaring says, 'It's as though the Pandanus grew up in the crevice. Like the water, there's a sense that it has always been there'.

PHOTOGRAPHY BY GRAHAM MELTZER, JOHN MAINWARING

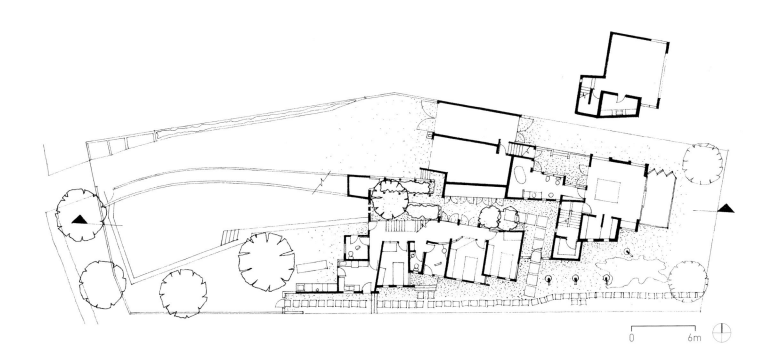

0 ⊕ 6m

# CALMING WATERS

## GRODSKI ARCHITECTS

This new house, by Grodski Architects, was designed for artist Debbie Sheezel. Her brief was for a separate studio, which was distinct but well-connected to the main house and garden. 'Debbie was moving from a large family home. Her previous house had a studio, but there was no connection to the garden,' says architect Russell Casper.

The new house replaced a 1920's bungalow and included a large aluminium-clad studio at the front of the property. Accessed immediately inside the front entrance, it looks out to a tranquil Japanese-style courtyard, which features a central pond filled with fish and waterlilies. Surrounded by pebbles, the view is meditative. To one side of the courtyard, screening the view into the main living area, is a 3.5-metre slate wall with cascading water. 'Our client wanted a direct view into the garden. But privacy from the street and the main house was also important,' says Casper.

Behind the slate wall is a pond, 4.5 metres long, 1.2 metres wide and 250 millimetres deep. Filled with black river pebbles, the pond appears as an extension to the slate wall. 'You can't see into the courtyard from the living area. The wall was designed to create separate experiences,' says Casper, who included a large European-style garden in the back of the house to create another different experience.

Water is integral to this home; included for its calming nature, it also adds drama to spaces. As Casper says, 'Debbie spends a considerable amount of time in her studio. We wanted her to feel as if she was part of this landscape'.

PHOTOGRAPHY BY SHARYN CAIRNS

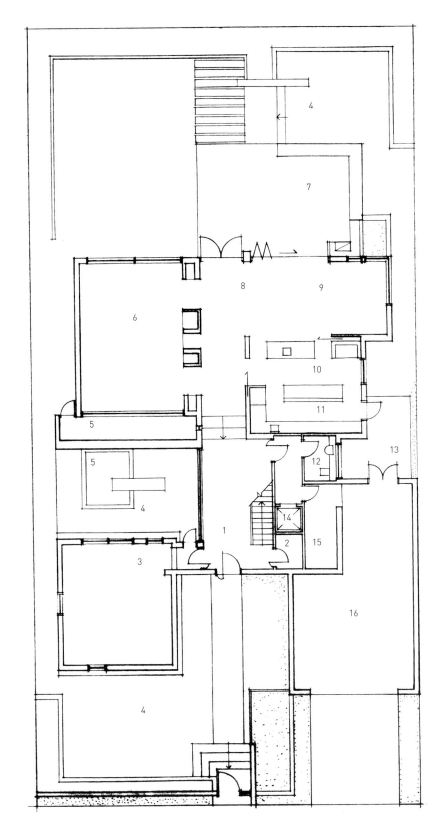

| | | | |
|---|---|---|---|
| 1 | Entry | 9 | Meals |
| 2 | Coat | 10 | Kitchen |
| 3 | Studio | 11 | Pantry |
| 4 | Courtyard | 12 | Powder room |
| 5 | Pond | 13 | Service yard |
| 6 | Living | 14 | Lift |
| 7 | Terrace | 15 | Store |
| 8 | Dining | 16 | Garage |

# CAPTURING THE LANDSCAPE

## INARC ARCHITECTS PTY LTD

Set in an indigenous landscape, this three-level house in a leafy suburb overlooks a river. Constructed of concrete, dark bronze aluminium, glass and bluestone, the house makes a heroic gesture against the established gum trees. The land was excavated to anchor the home – designed by architect Reno Rizzo and interior designer Christopher Hansson of Inarc Architects – in its bushland setting. Landscape architect Robert Boyle worked with Inarc to create the meandering rock garden that features a naturalistic-style fishpond.

The site was excavated to create three levels. The garage, workshop, office and guest bedrooms, together with an art studio and media room are located on the ground level. The first floor has a second bedroom, kitchen, dining and living area that leads to a large patio directly above the media room. The main bedroom and ensuite occupy the third level. Water cascading over basalt boulders starts at street level and works its way down, forming a small pond, filled with goldfish and water lilies. The basalt rocks appear to have come from the nearby riverbed, but were transported from some distance. Bluestone paving adjacent to the pond creates a dramatic internal courtyard.

The main passage on the ground floor looks directly into the courtyard. 'You're always reminded of the water every time you enter one of the rooms on the ground floor. The sound, as well as the sight is always there,' says Rizzo, who ensured the water could also be appreciated from the terrace outside the main living area and from the main bedroom. In the rear garden is a small spa pool. 'One body of water is deliberately man-made, while the pond has an organic form,' he adds. To maximise the view of the pond from the outdoor terrace, the architects included a clear toughened glass balustrade in the design.

Mixed with a green oxide, the home's concrete takes on the natural hues of the bush. As Rizzo says, 'You're reminded of the bush wherever you stand, inside or outside the house. But you can also see water, whether it's in the pond or the river nearby'.

PHOTOGRAPHY BY PETER CLARKE

# CONNECTIONS TO WATER

KEITH PIKE ASSOCIATES

This three-level property was designed by Keith Pike and his partner Catherine Whitty. Located on a modest 230-square-metre site with views of a harbour, there are visual and aural connections to water both within and beyond the site.

The sound of water greets visitors before they have entered the property. Inside the front gate, a small Japanese-inspired garden creates a calm environment. The source of the sound becomes apparent as water spills into the linear pond stocked with Japanese carp. The transparency of the frameless glass front entry provides an immediate connection to the plunge pool in the rear garden, visible through the body of the house.

Pike studied under Kazuo Shinohara at the Tokyo Institute of Technology, before working with the renowned architect Arata Isozaki. 'There was always a blurred interface between interior and exterior spaces in the work of the Japanese,' says Pike.

A pavilion-like home office and library sit at the rear of the house, opening to the garden and plunge pool. The living and dining areas occupy the second level and have been designed as an elevated pavilion with walls of glass opening onto both decks. Views of the city and harbour are exploited as borrowed landscape.

While the plunge pool is relatively small in scale (3.5 by 3.5 metres), like the city views, its presence in the home is considerably larger. The home's reflection in the pool creates a magnifying effect, as it appears to double in size. The pool also belies its depth of only 1.5 metres. 'The cobalt tiles create a perception of depth. At night there's a turquoise glow that reflects back into the upstairs living area,' says Pike. For Pike and Whitty, the water also sets up a journey through the property. 'The fishpond connects with the plunge pool. Then there's the view of the harbour through the treetops,' he adds.

PHOTOGRAPHY BY BRETT BOARDMAN

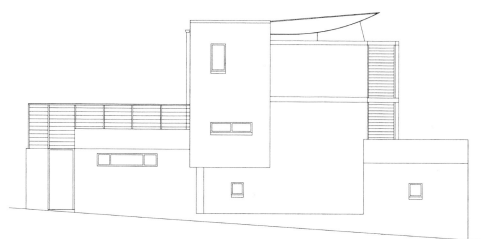

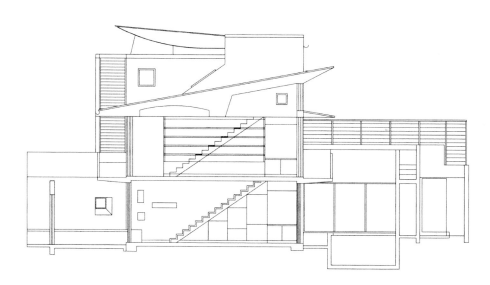

# DAPPLED LIGHT

### RICHARD SWANSSON ARCHITECT

This Victorian-style villa was previously a boarding house. Covered in layers of paint, the two-storey house sat in a well-established garden. 'My clients were quite specific. They still wanted the formal living and dining areas, but they wanted a completely new wing for the kitchen and casual living area,' says architect Richard Swansson.

Typical of many boarding houses, the design featured several kitchenettes, some of which were located on the enclosed verandah. A new kitchen, casual eating and living area were conceived as one large box attached to the original house. While the addition is contemporary, the scale and proportions of the new wing are sympathetic to the original Victorian design. The ceilings are approximately 4 metres high and the new walls are deliberately thick at 450 millimetres.

The 40-square-metre addition is designed with three sets of French doors to the pool and terrace area. Light reflecting from the pool bounces off the interior walls. 'Even the best photographer finds it difficult capturing that dappled effect on the walls,' says Swansson.

The pool was deliberately located in the corner of the site to allow the garden to be the focus from the street. The pool is positioned hard up against the rendered boundary wall and is downplayed by the black pebbles lining it. The pool illuminates the interior of the new wing. The owners can be in the kitchen with the doors open and also hear the sound of water from spouts embedded in the side rendered wall. As Swansson says, 'It's quite a magical space. You really only appreciate it once you're inside'.

PHOTOGRAPHY BY DEREK SWALWELL

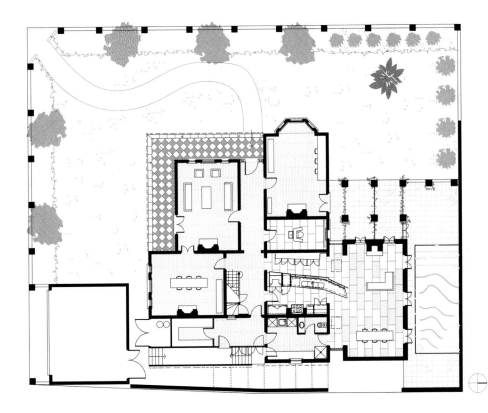

# DESIGNED AROUND THE POOL

48

This inner-city home is only a stone's throw from the beach. The owners originally lived next door in a small and narrow house and were delighted when the large adjacent site was up for sale.

Given the proximity of both the water and the city, it's not surprising that they were reluctant to move out of the neighbourhood.

Designed by Alex Popov Architects, the new concrete-rendered home is set around a large swimming pool. The C-shaped house features a living area at one end and three children's bedrooms at the other. The kitchen and dining area forms the back of the C, with the main bedroom and ensuite directly above on the first floor.

A series of monumental pillars frames the courtyard of the house. Large floor-to-ceiling glass doors are nestled behind these massive pillars. 'It's a contemporary version of an Arabian courtyard. But we kept the detail to a minimum. The central motif is the swimming pool. There's no need for additional decoration,' says architect Alex Popov, who was keen to contrast the home's white rendered walls with the brilliant blue of the water in the pool.

The only division between the outdoor patio and the swimming pool is a toughened-glass pool fence. For Popov, the pool is integral to the design and acts as an important cooling system within the home. 'The water acts as a heat exchange. The breeze carries the moisture from the pool and the sea into the home. During the warmer months, the doors are pulled right back'.

The courtyard design also reduced the perceived proximity of neighbouring homes. With the focus on the pool, rather than on backyards, there's increased privacy. 'The water also brings a sense of calm into the interior spaces. You can see it wherever you stand,' says Popov.

PHOTOGRAPHY BY KRAIG CARLSTROM

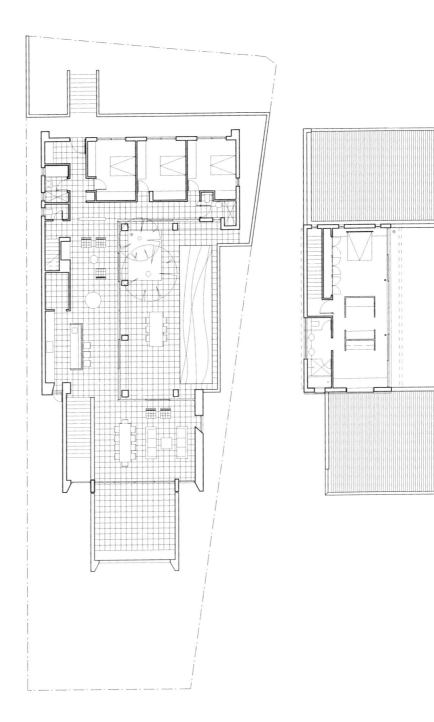

# THE ELEVATED POOL

## BIRD DE LA COEUR ARCHITECTS

This striking new home, on half a hectare of land, was designed by Bird de la Coeur Architects. Conceived around a central courtyard, the house includes three connecting wings, one of which is a kitchen, living and dining area. The pool, angled and elevated to capture the view of the bay, completes the square.

Designed for an extended family, Bird de la Coeur created a number of important divisions within the home. The spaces are defined by changes in floor levels and large sliding doors. 'The idea of thresholds was integral to the design. Even when a door leads off a corridor, it's never direct. You're aware of entering into someone else's space,' says architect Vanessa Bird, who included a number of plinths leading off the main passage to the various abodes.

The glazed living wing, which clips over the masonry wing, has spectacular views over the pool and the picturesque bay. While the postcard views and northern lights are idyllic, the architects were mindful of the harsher climate of the warmer months. Their alternative to the 'glass box' was to

create a contemporary style verandah in cedar. The cedar folds over the glass windows like a lid, creating sun protection and eliminating the occasional view of people walking along the cliff top.

Water frames an arid-style courtyard, forming the fourth side of a square. Designed by landscape architects, Rush Wright & Associates, the hardy coastal plantings are a contrast to the expansive pool. The 15-metre pool is elevated 1.4 metres above the ground and features a wet edge and black glass mosaic tiles. Being elevated above the ground eliminated the need for a pool fence. And for those using the pool, the elevation creates a sharper vista towards the headlands. The pool, as well as the bay, can also be appreciated from the living and dining areas of the house or alternatively from the generous verandahs.

Even when the weather turns, the movement of water in the pool can be appreciated. As Bird says, 'A pool should be functional all the time, whether it's actually used or simply seen from a number of vantage points within the house'.

PHOTOGRAPHY BY JOHN GOLLINGS, CATHERINE RUSH

# EXTENSIVE VIEWS

## GUZ ARCHITECTS

This house, designed by Guz Architects is located in Singapore, a place known for its tropical weather. 'We're extremely conscious of the need to create cool environments,' says architect Guz Wilkinson, who located the swimming pool on the third floor of this home. 'At this level, there's the breeze and the views of the neighbourhood'.

Designed for a developer, the site was subdivided to create two 465-square-metre allotments. The site is relatively deep and elevated at the rear by approximately 8 metres. 'We didn't see the point of putting a swimming pool at ground level. It would have been sandwiched between the neighbouring property and the home,' says Wilkinson.

On the ground floor of the house are the kitchen, living and dining areas. On the second level are the bedrooms. And on the third level is the family/television area, together with an additional bedroom. Above this area, creating a fourth level is the roof garden. The lap pool (approximately 20 metres long) also features a Jacuzzi with a glass front. 'The owners can sit in the Jacuzzi and look over the rooftops. This detail (glass front) can also be appreciated from the street,' says Wilkinson, who designed an open stairway to the roof to allow a more extensive view of the water. The balustrade surrounding the pool is made of steel wire, allowing an unimpeded view of the water and the neighbourhood.

In a tropical climate, any breeze is appreciated. As Wilkinson says, 'In land-scarce Singapore, the roof can be an inefficient use of space. We raised the whole pool and entertainment area up into the sky, making use of the views down into the valley below and the stronger breezes at the roof level'.

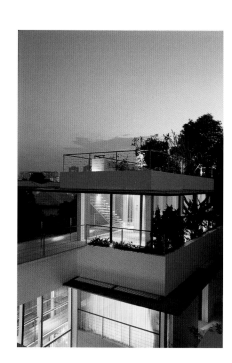

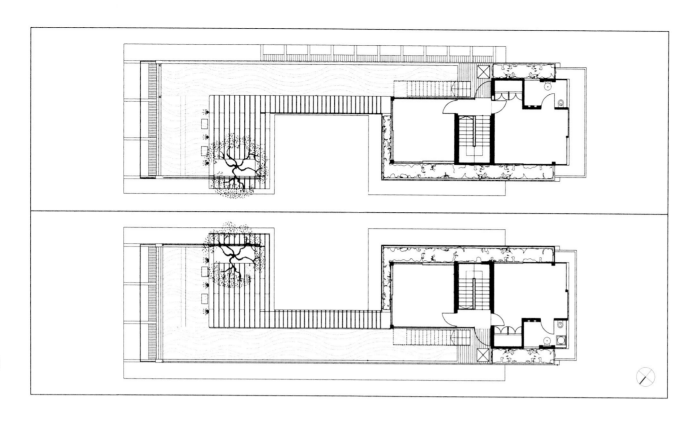

# FLOATING FORM

## SPACE AGENCY

This house, designed by architect Michael Patroni of the practice Space Agency, creates an impressive silhouette in the immediate area. A tennis court and swimming pool frame the soaring white forms of the house.

Located in a leafy suburb, one of the most appealing aspects is a 4-metre slope over the 90-metre length of the site. 'We took the approach that the project would set up its own internal aspect, where the project develops the whole site rather than just the house situated on the block,' says Patroni.

The boundary between the inside and outside of the house has been deliberately blurred. Different levels allow one space to 'float' while another space seems to be firmly anchored to the ground. The living areas, for example, extend beyond the pivotal timber doors and terrace down past the swimming pool, via a lily pond that reveals itself as the roof of the pavilion to the tennis court. The water garden surrounding the home is drawn into the interior using low windows at floor level. The reflected light of the moving water animates the interior spaces and emphasises the 'floating' quality of the house.

PHOTOGRAPHY BY ROBERT FRITH

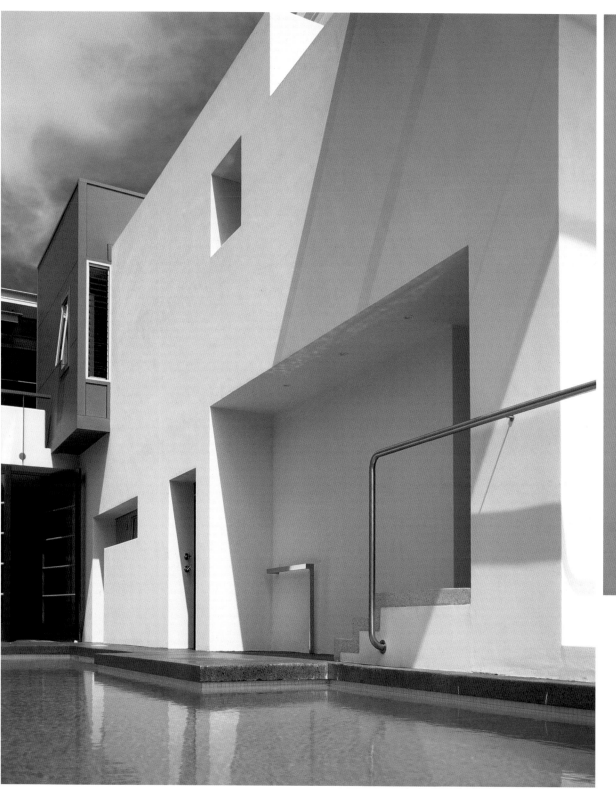

1 Bed
2 Dressing
3 Void
4 Sitting
5 Balcony

# AN INDOOR POOL

## SECCULL ARCHITECTS

Built in the 1970s, this brick house has several salient features and well-built generous spaces. Renovated by architect Martine Seccull a few years ago, the owners were ready for the next phase in the home's evolution, an indoor pool.

The house had a kidney-shaped pool in the central courtyard but it was exposed to the elements. 'My clients love to swim every day. The weather is unpredictable. The shape of the pool wasn't conducive to swimming laps,' says Seccull, who was commissioned to design the indoor pool and reconfigure the existing outdoor area.

Seccull lined the original kidney-shaped pool with concrete piers and put a concrete slab on top. The new structure is 3 by 5 metres and a pond is elevated 0.5 metres above ground, with a garden at its centre. The edge of the garden/pond is made of honed bluestone. 'When the weather is fine, chairs and table are brought out. The edge of the pond doubles as extra seating,' says Seccull.

The architect created a new garage and pool area in place of the original garage. The site was excavated 2.5 metres to allow for the new additions. Seccull rebuilt the pool wing in a style sympathetic with the original home. 'The pool wing structure is framed in steel. We've tried to match up the same brickwork that was used in the house,' says the architect, who was mindful of using materials such as brick to avoid the problems with condensation. The pool has a wet deck edge. Water from the pool simply disappears through slots on the edge of the pool. 'It sounds like you're standing under a waterfall,' she says. The wet deck edge creates a continuous vista with the surrounding landscape.

While the generous glass walls surrounding the pool are fixed, the central courtyard can be accessed through full-length glass concertinaed doors. The 6-metre opening also allows fresh air into the pool area.

PHOTOGRAPHY BY SHANIA SHEGEDYN

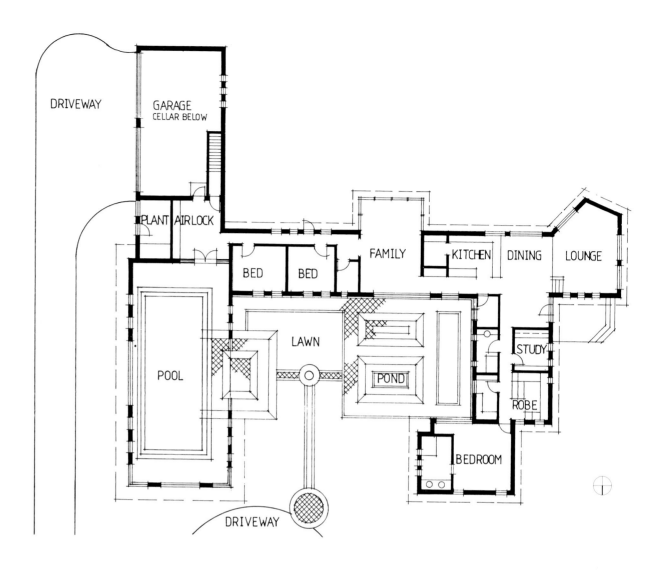

# INDOOR ROCK POOL

## WOODHEAD INTERNATIONAL PTY LTD

Designed by architect John Henry of Woodhead International, this warehouse-style home was originally no more than a farm-shed. Bought as a kit, the house is made of steel portal frames and corrugated iron. However, given the 15-degree slope of the land and the architect's desire for soaring volumes (7.5 metres), the shed required modification. Henry included a band of windows at ground level. And for heat retention, as well as protection, the fibreglass roof was lined with aluminium coating and a Dacron blanket. 'The design is based on the Venturi system. Cool air is drawn into the house from the windows and sucked through the vents in the ceiling. There's a continual movement of air,' says Henry.

Inspired by a house designed by Australian architect Robin Boyd in the late 1960s, (known as the Featherston House), Henry's open plan warehouse-style house overlooks a leafy gully and is surrounded by water. A pond and a waterfall are at the entrance to the home. Constructed of granite field boulders, the idea was to suggest arriving at the opening of a gully.

Inside, water appears in the form of a large 3 by 2.2-metre rock pool. Located at ground level at the rear of the house, the rock pool, also made of granite boulders, is filled with water plants and fish. Water flows over the rocks, appearing to emanate from the rock pool at the entrance. With the home elevated on a series of concrete platforms, there's a sense of water running under the house, from the front door to the back yard. Henry designed a cantilevered steel seat and steel mesh floor over the rock pool as a viewing platform.

Only the soaring glass wall at the rear of the house separates the internal rock pool from the spa pool on the other side. With the assistance of a pumping system, water from the spa finds its way into a larger dam-style rock pool (4 by 2 metres) that can be used for swimming. 'The water cools down the house by a few degrees. It's also quite refreshing and soothing,' says Henry. 'I've always admired the work of (Australian) landscape architect Gordon Ford. It's about the bush and living closely with it'.

PHOTOGRAPHY BY KIRSTY CHALMERS

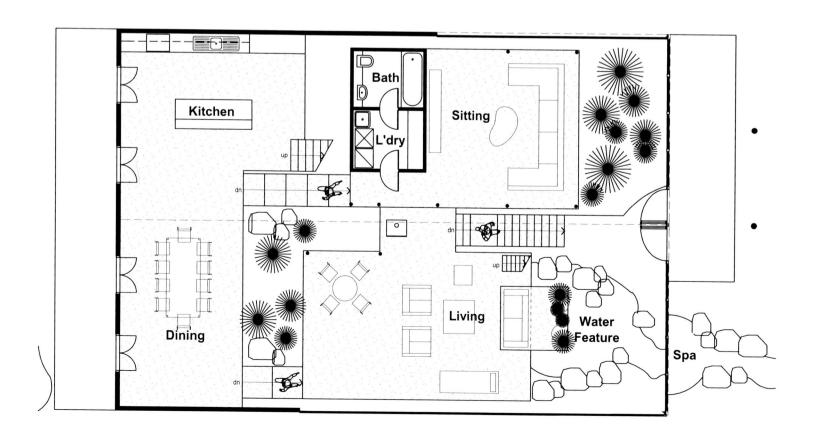

# A JAPANESE-STYLE POND

## DAVID LUCK ARCHITECTURE

Architect David Luck was commissioned to design a new wing for this 1930's English revival-style home. Luck retained the front of the house, which included a pitched roof and attic rooms and added a new kitchen, dining and living area, together with a Japanese-style tearoom.

Situated in an established garden, the tearoom lies in a deep pocket of shade. 'The tearoom was designed to reach out and sit in the centre of the garden,' says Luck. The tearoom appears as a separate pavilion and takes the form of two copper-clad shells, elevated 0.5 metres above ground level. Slotted-glass windows at ground level offer views of a pond and dense garden planting. A glass skylight dissecting the copper shells provides views of the sky.

The tearoom, approximately 4.5 metres in diameter, features bay windows on either side of the pavilion and French doors to the back garden. But it's the bridge between the tearoom and the kitchen, fully enclosed by glass, that causes the owners and guests to stop and reflect. The pond is approximately 6 metres in length, but its presence appears substantial. Viewed from all aspects of the new wing and the tearoom, the water adds a tranquil ambience to the design. The pond also connects to the timber deck outside the main living area. 'The pond allows light to reflect on the living room walls and ceilings,' says Luck, who also included a waterspout in the pond. 'I wanted to make the tearoom special. It was about creating a journey. You feel as if you are walking into the garden,' he adds.

PHOTOGRAPHY BY SHANIA SHEGEDYN

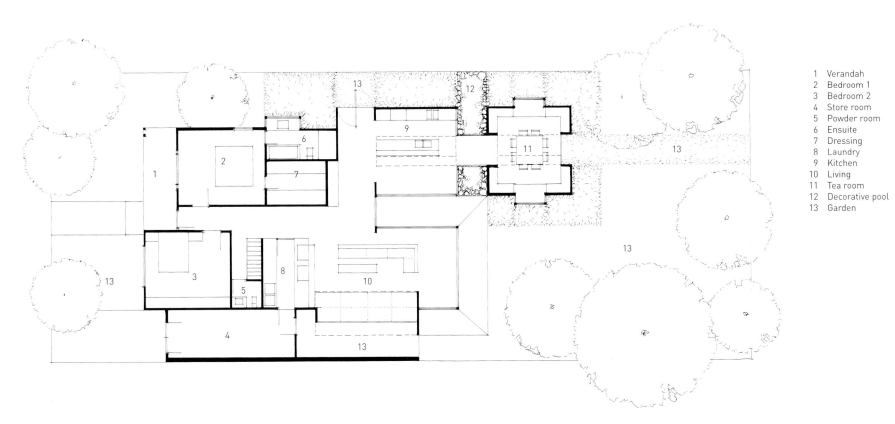

1 Verandah
2 Bedroom 1
3 Bedroom 2
4 Store room
5 Powder room
6 Ensuite
7 Dressing
8 Laundry
9 Kitchen
10 Living
11 Tea room
12 Decorative pool
13 Garden

# L-SHAPED POOL

## TOSCANO ARCHITECTS

This large period home located in a leafy suburb was originally used as a hostel for the Salvation Army. When the owners purchased the house, 'They wanted informal living and dining areas. They also needed additional bedrooms for their children,' says architect Joe Toscano.

While the original building was extensively reworked and restored, a completely separate wing was added, including a basement car park. 'We endeavoured to complement the original materials with those used in the new building,' says Toscano, who incorporated red brickwork and terracotta roof tiles in the addition.

Linking the original building to the new wing is an elliptical-shaped domed hall. 'It's the nodal entry point and links both wings to the tennis court,' says Toscano. An L-shaped pool, a major priority, was designed for the rear garden. The pool appears to merge with an adjacent pond. 'The pool is designed with the wet edge. The edges of the two pools of water are deliberately blurred,' he adds. Large bluestone tiles surround the pond, further diffusing the lines between the pathway and pond.

At the front of the house, outside the new dining room, is a reflective pool of water. Located above the carport that leads to the basement car park, this body of water creates a pensive and reflective mood in the dining room. Skylights in the dining room bring light into the space, with dappled light reflecting from the shallow pool of water. As Toscano says, 'The two bodies of water (front and rear gardens) are aligned. The water appears to run under the house'.

PHOTOGRAPHY BY TREVOR MEIN

# LAP POOL

## ODDEN RODRIGUES ARCHITECTS

This house is located near the city's largest river. Approximately 4 kilometres from town, the relatively large site is bound by a series of right of ways. 'There's only one boundary to a neighbouring home. It meant there weren't the normal setback issues with Council,' says architect Simon Rodrigues.

As the owners are avid readers of architectural magazines, they presented the architects with a sketch plan. While the scheme required considerable refinement, some of its hallmarks were later included in the architects' design. The curved wall, separating the kitchen and casual living areas from the more formal living areas, was retained in the final design. 'They also wanted some generous volumes in the design,' says Rodrigues, who included 3.6-metre-high ceilings on part of the ground floor. 'The higher volumes on the ground level meant we had to taper the roof planes,' he adds. The curved wall also divides the orthogonal spaces from the more angular ones. As a result, some of the rooms appear to have been 'cranked' in and out of the roof plain.

Outside the kitchen and informal living areas is a courtyard with a pergola. A metal canopy overhangs from the roof, creating added protection from the sun. Hard up against the boundary, to maximise the external space, is a lap pool, measuring 25 by 2.4 metres. Framing the pool is a limestone block wall, forming a boundary fence, contrasted with a local stonewall on another side. 'The large limestone blocks add an interesting dimension to the scale of the pool. Particularly when they are juxtaposed with the smaller bricks,' says Rodrigues.

Adjacent to the pool is a narrow strip of concrete pavers inside the pool fence. And beyond the fence is a small patio with a grassed area. While the owners appreciate the pool from inside the home during the day, they also derive pleasure from the water at night. The metal canopy that overhangs the roof reflects the water. As Rodrigues says, 'The water animates the entire façade. It's continually changing'.

PHOTOGRAPHY BY ROBERT FRITH AND ADRIAN LAMBERT

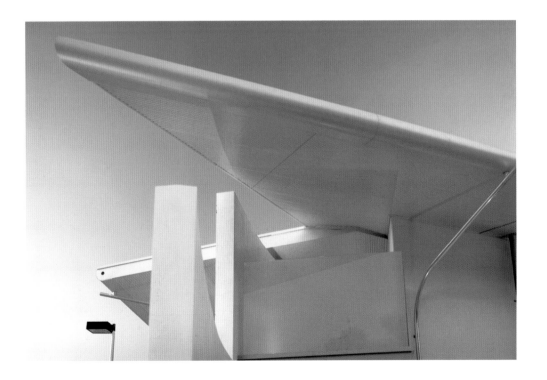

# LAP POOL WITHIN CUBE CLUSTER

ALEX POPOV ARCHITECTS

Designed by Alex Popov Architects, this house is located on a compact irregular site. Faced with severe council restrictions on what could be built, Popov elevated the home on a concrete plateau. The cube-like geometric spaces within the home centre on an 11-metre lap pool. 'It's really four cubes that have been clustered into two pavilions,' says Popov. One pavilion comprises the kitchen and main living area with bedrooms on the first floor. The other pavilion consists of the outdoor patio/rotunda. Elevating the pavilions above ground level also allowed for valuable parking space.

The presence of water is established immediately inside the front door. A double-storey void in the entrance features a soaring glass window wall, looking directly into the lap pool. The lap pool is also an integral feature of the main living area. Floor-to-ceiling glass doors can be pulled right back during the warmer months. The toughened glass balustrades that frame the pool provide the only separation between the pool and the living space. The children's bedrooms upstairs also enjoy views over the lap pool, with each bedroom cantilevering over the water.

As the weather permits alfresco dining, the architects included a generous outdoor patio. Open at the sides, and featuring a cut out roof, the outdoor pavilion creates a spacious feeling in the home. 'This area is a transitional space. You're aware that you are outside, but the canopy creates a sense of protection,' says Popov.

While the house is relatively modest in scale, approximately 300 square metres, it appears considerably larger, with the lap pool extending the site lines. From the street, this steel and concrete house also appears considerably monumental. As Popov says, 'Even though our building envelope was greatly reduced, we weren't prepared to compromise on the design'.

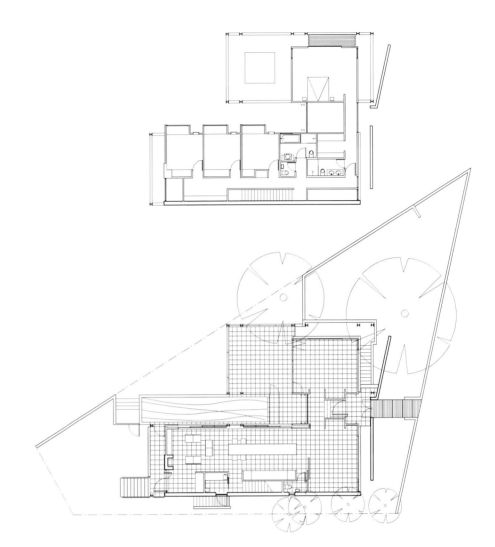

# AN OASIS IN THE CITY

BATES SMART
HPA PTY LTD

LAND DESIGN PARTNERSHIP
INCORPORATING CHRIS DANCE LAND DESIGN

Designed by Bates Smart and HPA Pty Ltd, these striking apartments occupy what was once a hospital site. Located on the edge of town in the main arts precinct, the residential towers provide a welcome addition to the changing skyline.

More than 200 apartments are on this site, spread over three towers and a row of terrace-style townhouses. While each apartment features generous balconies, the architects were also keen to provide a green oasis at the city's edge. 'Most of the residents were moving from large homes with established gardens. They didn't want to feel dislocated by moving into a harsh urban environment,' says landscape architect Chris Dance, who designed the external spaces with landscape architect Greg Hocking.

Both the architects and landscape architects extensively researched their market. Dance and Hocking for example, visited many of the suburbs that the residents were leaving. Many of the gardens they visited in these established middle-distance suburbs were the work of significant 20th-century landscape designers: Hilda Marriott, Edna Walling and Grace Fraser. 'We thought that

the design for the apartments should act as a tribute to these significant designers,' says Dance.

The main courtyard features a series of waterways that 'slice' through the glass windows and into the main foyer/lift area. 'We wanted to bring the landscape into the building. And because of the scale of the building, the water features are deliberately over-scale,' says Hocking. Land Design Partnership included heavy planting on the periphery of the site. They also designed a dramatic sweeping pergola. Made of steel, the pergola offers privacy from those looking down from above. 'We saw the canopy like a picket fence. It has just been manipulated for a new environment,' says Dance, who worked closely with the architects on the project.

Water appears in several swimming pools, in the channels of water slicing through the courtyard and in the shallow bodies of water framing the apartments. As Dance says, 'We wanted to bring the landscape into the building. But we didn't want to create a conservatory. It's an urban space and we've responded in a contemporary way. But we've also made a connection to the past'.

# ON THE BANKS OF A CANAL

HULENA ARCHITECTS

This house sits on the banks of a canal. Located in a small beachside settlement on the North Island of New Zealand, this house offers an escape for the owners whose primary residence is in Auckland. 'They wanted a weekender that was a contrast to their period-style home in the city. The brief required a completely different form, one that was considerably more open to the elements,' says architect Brent Hulena.

The new house, constructed of glass and stone, features a flat roof made of zinc. The materials, as well as the form of this house, contrast with the traditional pitched-roofed homes on the estate. 'The concept is a pavilion. It's essentially a glazed box, a stone's throw from the beach,' says Hulena. The house is L-shaped. The main wing facing the canal comprises the kitchen, living and dining area, together with the main bedroom. The other wing includes four other bedrooms. While the house is relatively moderate in size

(approximately 250 square metres), the height of the ceilings (3.5 metres) creates a sense of space.

The living areas face the front terrace, the lap pool and canal on one side and an internal courtyard on the other. The pool is elevated 2.5 metres above the canal, offering water views to the home's interior spaces as well as providing the owners a view of the canal and all its activities. 'You feel as if you're actually swimming in the canal when you're swimming in the pool,' says Hulena, who included a narrow grass patch between the canal and the lap pool. 'I wanted to ensure there was some division,' he adds.

Unlike the owner's city home that features traditional windows, the floor-to-ceiling windows offer direct access to the terrace and pool. As Hulena says, 'It's continual theatre. There's always movement in the water, whether it's in the lap pool or in the canal'.

PHOTOGRAPHY BY PATRICK REYNOLDS

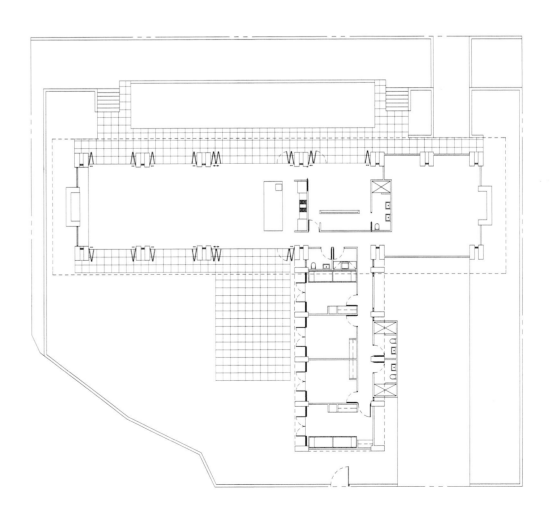

# A PARTY

## ALLAN POWELL ARCHITECTS

This house, designed by Allan Powell Architects, was inspired by the 1960's film *The Party*, starring the late Peter Sellers. The other influence in the house is North Africa, a place the owners frequently visit. 'The house featured in *The Party* is high modernism. It's extremely fluid and celebrates the most exuberant point of this period,' says architect Allan Powell.

The house comprises two levels with an additional basement car park and rumpus room. The ground level features the kitchen, dining and living areas, together with a bar. The bedrooms are on the first floor. The curvaceous cement-rendered building wraps around a lap pool, rectilinear in shape. There is a separate hot spa and steam room adjacent to the pool. 'The house and the pool are deliberately juxtaposed,' says Powell.

The exterior render is raw and earthy in colour, while the interior and external columns are flamboyant. Columns on the terrace are finished with scarlet-red glass mosaic tiles, as in the kitchen. The interior is deliberately luscious and features a rich and eclectic melange of materials. The exterior is considerably more primitive. Evocative of tent-like structures in North Africa, the terrace includes a timber pergola, complete with canvas curtains that can be drawn across to create an 'outdoor' room. When the curtains are tied back, reflections from the water appear on the ceiling in the living areas.

Water also features at the entrance of the home. Just like the guests in *The Party*, visitors are required to walk over stepping-stones to reach the front door. For Powell, the brief wasn't simply an opportunity to recreate a legendary interior, it was a chance to work with clients who wanted to celebrate high design in the 21st century, decades after the film was made. As Powell says, 'It's like visiting a luxury hotel in Marrakech. But in this case, the clients can stay as long as they wish'.

PHOTOGRAPHY BY JOHN GOLLINGS

# THE PENTHOUSE POOL

## SJB INTERIORS

The inner-city penthouse was designed by Andrew Parr, a director of SJB Interiors, for a couple leaving a large family home. As a result, the design focuses on fewer bedrooms and increased living and entertaining areas. And even though a large manicured garden was left behind in the suburbs, Parr has designed a generous balcony that wraps around the entire apartment, one elevation including a 12-metre-long lap pool.

To accentuate the view to the city, the kitchen has been deliberately pared back. Central to the stainless steel kitchen is a Calacutta marble island bench. Apart from a commercial cooler for wine, everything else is concealed, from the refrigerator to the dishwasher. Also pared back is the dining area. The main focus here is the lap pool, which is framed by an elevated bluestone wall. Clear toughened glass along the edge of the lap pool acts as a balustrade. The glass also reflects the sky and neighbouring vistas of palm trees.

In the centre of a 17-metre span across the living area is an enclosed media room, lined with Madagascar ebony. With circular red suede banquette-style seating and a silk-covered wall that frames the video and entertainment unit, the space can be completely enclosed. 'It's a contained pod in the centre of the glazed space,' says Parr, who compares the interior to a luxurious hotel. 'People looking at penthouses want a lot more than just a view. They want a large bathroom, a walk-in wardrobe and generous main bedroom,' says Parr. 'Some also want their own pool, rather than just shared facilities,' he adds.

PHOTOGRAPHY BY TONY MILLER

# PERCHED ON A CLIFF

## BRIAN MEYERSON ARCHITECTS PTY LTD

Designed by Brian Meyerson Architects, this house occupies a unique site overlooking the Pacific Ocean. While the site is breathtaking, the original late-1970's home was less impressive. 'It was a project-style home. It didn't relate to the ocean. It really could have been built anywhere,' says architect Brian Meyerson.

The current design was the result of a limited competition among the local architects. The brief to all four practices was to retain as much of the original home as possible, space for three cars and a lap pool. The clients also wanted the renovation to not only relate to the ocean, but also to evoke a sense of serenity and isolation, though located in a built-up area.

Instead of the house screaming for attention from the street, it is well concealed on the battleaxe-shaped site. Approached by a laneway, the entrance features a boardwalk-style path leading through the house to the pool and ocean in the distance. 'The further you enter the house, the more the views to the ocean open up,' says

Meyerson. The first floor of the house consists of garaging for three cars, a combined dining and living area overlooking the pool, an enclosed courtyard and a pavilion beyond, used for a gymnasium. On the first floor are bedrooms and a small studio. 'The pavilion provides shelter to the courtyard. But it also creates privacy from a neighbouring home,' says Meyerson. 'In this space, you feel as though you're in a helicopter. There's an 80-metre drop to the ocean,' he adds.

While some of the original walls and floors were retained in the renovation, the design reads as a completely new house. With deep revers for sunlight protection and generous glass walls, there is little connection to the original 1970's home. A generous bank of louvred-glass windows covering the breadth of the kitchen and living areas cools the house on warmer days. Wind carries moisture from the lap pool to the open-plan spaces. As Meyerson says, 'We tucked the lap pool right up against the edge of the house so the sound of water can also be appreciated from the living spaces'.

PHOTOGRAPHY BY BRETT BOARDMAN AND BRIAN MEYERSON

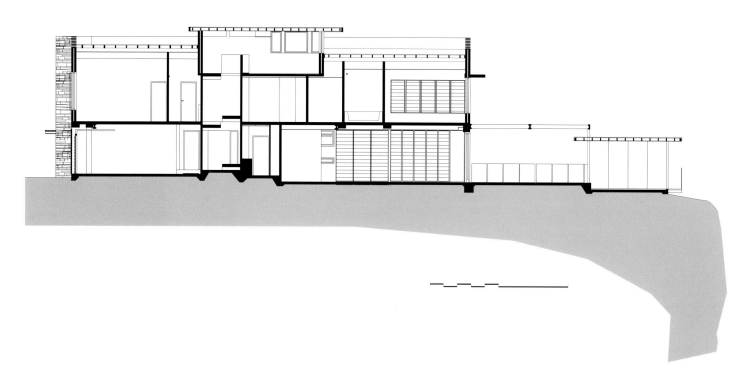

# A PRIVATE POOL

HAYBALL LEONARD STENT PTY LTD ARCHITECTS

This pool, measuring 7 by 3.5 metres, is directly outside the master bedroom. On hot summer nights, the doors can be pulled right back and the owners can jump directly into the pool. 'The water also keeps the temperature down,' says architect Rob Stent, who lives in the house with his wife and teenage children. 'The pool was something the children were keen to have. They were prepared to have less garden space. And anyway, we're near a park,' adds Stent.

The Victorian terrace was originally a cacophony of services and lean-tos. Stent, director of Hayball Leonard Stent Architects, opened up the two front rooms to create a main bedroom and ensuite. A new kitchen, dining and living space were added, together with children's quarters on the first floor. The shotgun corridor that runs down one side of the cottage was incorporated into the main living area and now overlooks the swimming pool.

Directly outside the main living area is a courtyard that leads to the swimming pool. However, while there's direct access to the pool from the main bedroom, the pool can also be seen from the main living area and from the secondary living space, used by the children. 'It is integral to the renovation. It wasn't just an afterthought,' says Stent.

Framing the pool and creating privacy to the street, is a high slatted-timber fence, made of a variety of hardwoods. Some battens have been varnished while others have been left in their raw state, to create a ripple effect, not dissimilar to the water in the pool. The screen-like fence also conceals the pool equipment, which is nestled behind. However, Stent was keen to provide a glimpse of the original Victorian front verandah. A small gap between the timber and rendered wall offers an intimate view. 'I wanted to make a connection between the original and the new work,' says Stent.

As well as providing a focal point for the interior spaces, the water also cools the home. Doors are left open and moist air from the pool is carried though the open-plan design. As Stent says, 'Water has a magical effect when it reacts with sunlight. The patterns on the walls and ceilings are truly a visual delight'.

PHOTOGRAPHY BY SHANNON MCGRATH

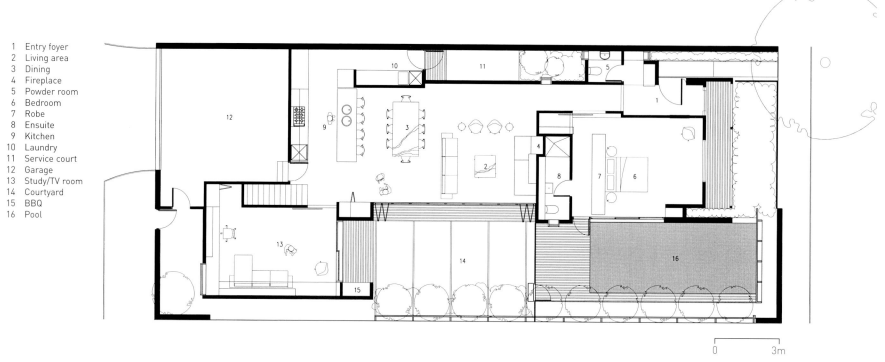

1 Entry foyer
2 Living area
3 Dining
4 Fireplace
5 Powder room
6 Bedroom
7 Robe
8 Ensuite
9 Kitchen
10 Laundry
11 Service court
12 Garage
13 Study/TV room
14 Courtyard
15 BBQ
16 Pool

0        3m

117

# RAINFOREST MAGIC

### GUZ ARCHITECTS

This large home, designed by Guz Architects, is orientated towards dense rainforest. Located at the end of a road, the architects were keen to turn away from the neighbouring homes and public areas. To achieve this Guz Architects designed this large three-storey home (approximately 900 square metres) in two wings. 'We had to crank up one of the wings to allow a fuller of view of the forest,' says architect Guz Wilkinson. One wing includes the kitchen and dining area. The other wing comprises the living area. The bedrooms are spread over the two wings. The gap between the two wings forms the courtyard/entrance to this impressive home.

Both the owners and architects were keen to include water at the entrance to the home. The owners also wanted a lush green lawn. 'We designed an island-style courtyard,' says Wilkinson, who included a shallow moat surrounding the lawn. The lawn is accessed by strategically placed stepping stones in the moat.

As the site is on a steep slope, the architects were able to include a basement level in the house, together with a substantial pool. The pool finishes 3 metres beyond the edge of the dining area above and includes a Jacuzzi. There's also a billiard/rumpus room at the basement level. As it is located in a tropical environment, the architects included a watery area away from the harsh sunlight. Protected by a cantilevered balcony that leads from the dining area, the owners can sit in the Jacuzzi for extended periods of time.

While the pool can be enjoyed from the garden, it can also be appreciated from the cantilevered balconies that lead from the dining area and main bedroom. Wire balustrades on both balconies allow for an unimpeded view of the water. The shallow moat surrounding the courtyard acts as a cooling device, with the wind drawing the moisture through the lower levels of the house. Dotted with water features, the moat offers a pleasant ambience for arriving guests.

PHOTOGRAPHY BY LUCA INVERNIZZI TETTONI

# REFLECTING THE LIGHT

## DURBACH BLOCK ARCHITECTS

Designed by Durbach Block Architects, this house features a 35-metre-long water garden. An oval-shaped pool, which extends the length of the house, is less than 300 millimetres deep. A walkway through the middle of the water garden, which is filled with fish, water lilies and irises, leads to an elevated courtyard.

The pool was primarily designed to increase the amount of light coming into the home, in particular, the bedrooms on the ground level. 'Light reflects off the water and into the house. The light animates the interior,' says architect Neil Durbach.

The white concrete and masonry house parallels the curves of the pond. And while some water features are an afterthought, this pond is integral to the design. 'Our clients realised that the orientation of the site would restrict their landscape plans. But they were keen to create an environment where plants would easily grow,' says Durbach.

Creating a unique environment, as well as finding a solution for practical concerns was also on the minds of the architects. The water can moderate the temperature in the home, both on the ground level and in the kitchen and living areas on the first floor. Water was also a way to both energise and create a sense of calm within the house.

But while there's pleasure from living with water, there are certain problems that can be associated with it. 'Leakages can be a problem and the construction of watercourses can be quite complex. We always work closely with a landscape architect. There really aren't any short cuts,' says Durbach. And while the sight and sound of water can greatly enhance the home, it needs to be fully integrated into the design. As Durbach says, 'Sometimes using water can just be a meaningless exercise. And there's nothing worse than a stagnant pool of water. It's more than just creating a decorative feature for the sake of creating a point of difference'.

# A RIVER BED

MCGAURAN GIANNINI SOON PTY LTD

This house appears to be adjacent to a riverbed. However, the meandering pebbled path along the side of the house merely suggests a river, because the only water that crosses the surface is rainwater. 'The pebbles are a reminder of the home's location, near the beach,' says architect Rob McGauran, who worked with landscape architects, Landarch, on this project.

The 400-square-metre house was designed for a large family seeking a sea change from their previous heritage home. 'They wanted a contemporary house. They didn't want a series of dark passages like they experienced in their former home,' says McGauran.

Instead of separate formal lounge and dining rooms at the front of the house, McGauran Giannini Soon designed a large 'floating' glass box. Framed in steel, the window across the side boundary is at ground level. Designed to allow display of the owner's artwork and for privacy from the neighbouring house, the lowered window offers views of the pebbled path.

The kitchen and open casual living area are located at the rear of the home, with direct access to the rear garden, while the bedrooms are upstairs. The architects were keen to include an outdoor room leading to the garden. Like a verandah, the outdoor room has timber on the walls, floor and ceiling. Generous in size (3 metres deep and 3 metres high), the enclosed verandah/patio extends across the entire rear façade, allowing uninterrupted views of the lawn and pool.

The pool, which is enclosed by clear toughened glass, features striking black tiles with a white tiled cross. 'It's a flat site and we wanted to ensure the pool could be appreciated from several aspects within the house. There's also a clear view of the water from the bedrooms upstairs,' says McGauran. The cross in the pool also refers to the windows and structure of the house. 'We wanted to create a dialogue with the home's rectilinear design,' he adds.

PHOTOGRAPHY BY JOHN GOLLINGS

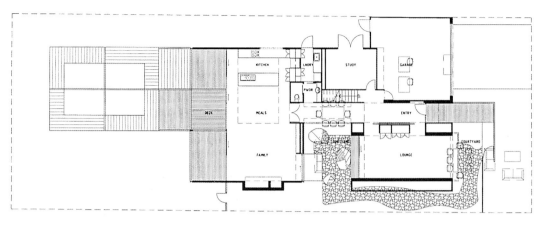

SITE AND GROUND FLOOR PLAN

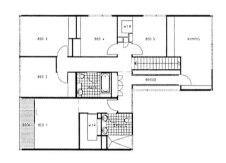

# SCULPTED WATER FEATURE

ALUDEAN

Designed by sculptors Lu Skacej and Dean Colls of Aludean, this courtyard features a striking pond and water feature. The duo, who were brought into the project by landscape designer Jack Merlo, were extensively briefed by the clients. 'The house was designed for a family with six children. They wanted a water feature that would create a sense of calm, even if the reality was sometimes otherwise,' says Skacej.

The watery courtyard can be seen immediately past the front door. The striking forms in the courtyard complement the clean lines of the home. The pond, framed by floor-to-ceiling windows, can be appreciated from the dining area and kitchen, as well as from the passage and entrance. 'The owners wanted quite a heraldic feel to the sculptured water feature. 'Something that indicated you'd arrived,' says Skacej.

The water feature comprises two black concrete monolithic forms, of differing size, together with a series of horizontal stainless steel shelves that fill up with water. The two materials intersect in a single form. At the base of the 3 by 3 metre pond are slate grey tiles, with goldfish moving freely under the cantilevered stainless beam. Each of the black concrete shapes overflows with water, the water being regulated in two speeds, one more restful, the other more charged. 'When the owners have a larger party, the water tends to be on the higher cycle,' says Skacej.

The sound of water makes an impact in the interior spaces, as does the artificial lighting in the 300-millimetre-deep pond. At night, the light plays with the water and creates unusual shadows on the rendered walls. To create texture in the composition, Aludean included a square concrete 'dish', filled with black pebbles.

PHOTOGRAPHY BY PETER CLARKE

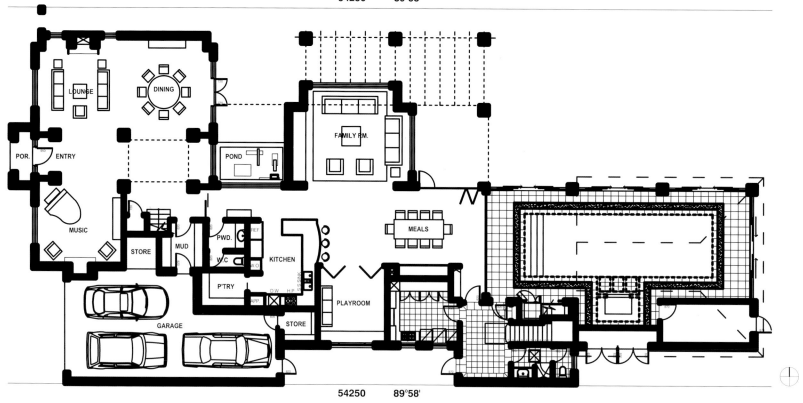

LOUNGE

DINING

FAMILY RM.

POND

POR.  ENTRY

MUSIC

STORE

MUD

PWD.

REF

W/C

KITCHEN

MEALS

P'TRY

APP

DW  HP

STORE

PLAYROOM

GARAGE

STORE

# A SENSE OF TRANQUILLITY

b.e. ARCHITECTURE

Designed for a couple with two small children, the brief to b.e. Architecture was to create a substantial house (approximately 400 square metres) that had a sense of permanence. 'Both our clients and ourselves didn't want to draw attention to a new house. The preference was to sit quietly among the other buildings in the street,' says Broderick Ely, who designed the house with architect Jonathan Boucher, a co-director of the practice.

Water makes its appearance immediately inside the high front fence of this home. A small fishpond with water plants greets visitors as they make their way along a verdant pathway lined with trees. The front door opens to reveal a generous internal courtyard with kitchen and living areas wrapped around a glazed light well. Through the formal living area beyond the courtyard there are views of the pool in the back garden.

The ground floor comprises an open plan kitchen, dining and living area, together with a small and elevated nook leading off the kitchen. The courtyard's glazed walls provide definition and there are subtle changes in the floor and ceiling levels in the home. The formal living area, for example, has marginally higher ceilings (250 millimetres) than the kitchen and dining area. Joinery placed at the edge of the living area creates a pathway from the back garden to the kitchen and dining spaces.

The water lapping from the pool against the glass walls on the rear façade creates a sense of tranquillity. 'We cut the pool into the living area by a metre. This wall is fixed. We didn't want the smell of chlorine entering the house,' says Ely, who installed a small ledge/seat adjacent to the living room wall, for both adults and children to relax and look back into the house. As the house is orientated to capture maximum sunlight, a substantial steel pergola extends the width of the rear façade. There is also a 6-metre steel built-in barbecue. As Ely says, 'When all the doors are pulled back, there's a gentle breeze through the house. And it's tinged with moisture and sometimes the familiar smell of outdoor cooking'.

1  Foyer
2  Bedroom
3  Bedroom
4  Terrace
5  Bedroom
6  Living
7  Courtyard below
8  Bedroom
9  Terrace
10 Pool/courtyard below

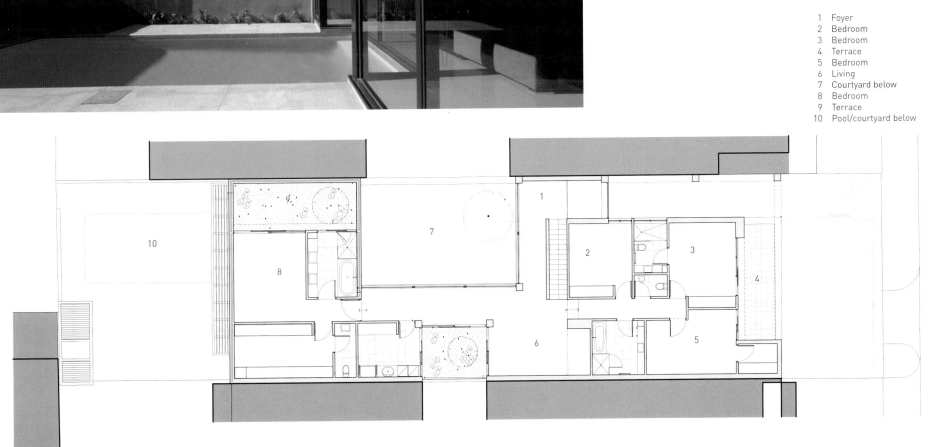

# SMALL POOL FOR EXERCISE

## O'CONNOR + HOULE ARCHITECTURE

This unusual home on the edge of town replaced a semi-detached house on a site that measured only 10 by 20 metres.

Mindful of its client's request for privacy and wanting to give something back to the street, O'Connor + Houle Architecture designed one façade to the street like a double skin. Corrugated fibreglass conceals the windows that are made of a German glass called 'dimant frost'. While the fibreglass makes a welcome addition to the streetscape during the day, at night the house reveals an inner glow. 'When illuminated from within, objects such as a steel-framed bookshelf reveal their form,' says architect Annick Houle.

On the ground floor of this home is the kitchen, dining and living area, together with an outdoor terrace and plunge pool. The first level contains the main bedroom, additional bedrooms, bathrooms and a second living area. 'One of the owners is a competitive swimmer. She wanted a pool even though the site was relatively small,' says architect Stephen O'Connor. The pool is only 1.5 by 4 metres in length, so swimming jets were included in the design so that she could swim against them.

The courtyard garden behind the front fence is rather small, so to compensate, the architects located the pool on the edge of the living area. 'The living areas were designed around the pool. The pool encroaches on the interior spaces,' says Houle. Polished concrete flooring in the kitchen and living areas extends to the outdoor terrace. 'The pool looks as if it has been cut out of the concrete,' says Holule.

Even though the owners applauded the architects' ingenuity when it came to certain materials, they didn't want to have any timber or stainless steel in the house. O'Connor and Houle suggested timber on the staircase to contrast with the concrete. When the owners wouldn't budge, they designed the staircase using solid steel tubes. Its twig-like form was their way of creating a 'forest' of steel.

*This house first appeared in 'Domain,'* The Age *Newspaper 27 September 2000*

145

# THE SOUND OF WATER

ARCHITECTS INK

This house, designed by Architects Ink, is on a large irregularly shaped site measuring 1285 square metres. As the site is skewed, the architects designed the house in a V-shape. One wing includes the kitchen and casual living area, with the bedrooms on the first floor. The other wing comprises the formal lounge. Between the two wings is the swimming pool.

'Our clients wanted a large house (approximately 500 square metres). They have two young boys. So they wanted sufficient room that also provided them with a sense of independence,' says architect Marc Spinelli. The children's bedroom leads directly onto the rumpus room upstairs. The parents' bedroom is at the opposite end of the corridor, a reasonable distance away.

There are extensive views of the swimming pool from various aspects within the house. The rumpus room for example, offers one of the most dramatic views of the swimming pool.

Cantilevered over the living area below, the floor of the rumpus room extends to form a canopy to the terrace. A small viewing platform, 600 millimetres wide, extends from the rumpus room and hovers above the pool. A glass-bottom floor, walls and ceiling create a floating effect for those standing within. A precast concrete panel partially conceals the viewing platform to ensure privacy, both for neighbours and the family.

The pool (9 by 4 metres) comes up to the perimeter of the dining area, flowing under the rumpus room above. 'The water looks as though it's slicing through the house,' says Spinelli, who was keen to make water integral to the architecture. A water feature at the end of the pool also resonates. The sound of water is amplified as it moves across the stainless steel shelves embedded in the boundary wall. 'Even if you're sitting in a room without water views, you know that it's just outside your door,' says Spinelli.

PHOTOGRAPHY BY TREVOR FOX

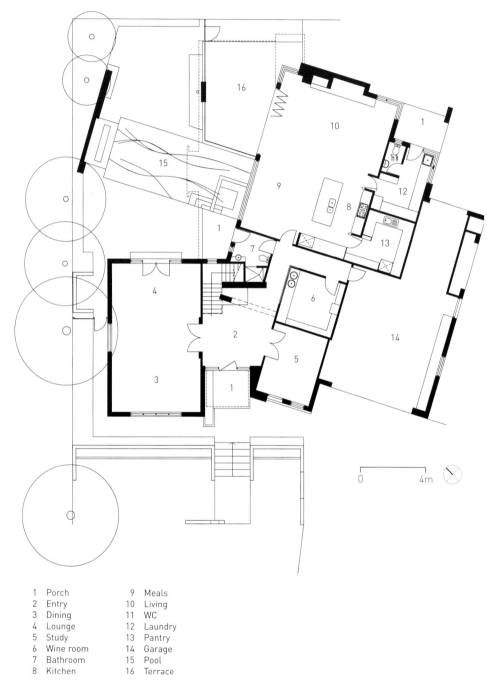

1  Porch
2  Entry
3  Dining
4  Lounge
5  Study
6  Wine room
7  Bathroom
8  Kitchen
9  Meals
10 Living
11 WC
12 Laundry
13 Pantry
14 Garage
15 Pool
16 Terrace

# SURROUNDED BY WATER

## VIRGINIA KERRIDGE ARCHITECT

This house on the harbour's edge is surrounded by water. While the view of the harbour was a drawcard to purchasing the site, the decline of approximately 30 metres certainly wasn't. 'We had to excavate the site quite extensively. Part of the council brief was to maintain the views of the harbour from the street,' says architect Virginia Kerridge who designed the house. From the street, one sees roofs cascading down to the water with the harbour in the distance.

The house is designed over five levels and Kerridge was keen to use a variety of materials. At harbour level, the materials are predominantly of formed concrete, while the main living area on the upper level is constructed of hardwood cladding and exposed steel. The garage is at street level. Below this level are the main kitchen, living and dining areas. A level below comprises the main bedroom, two additional bedrooms and a home cinema. Directly below are two additional bedrooms, a laundry and a sauna. The rumpus room/gymnasium is at harbour level.

Water from the harbour affects the interior spaces, depending on whether it's overcast and grey or sky-blue. Though the water is a considerable distance from the main living areas, the glazed walls are a reminder of the proximity of the water. 'It's like living in a tent. It's more akin to a shelter,' says Kerridge.

The pool is approximately 12 metres in length and the depth tapers from 8 to 6 metres. 'I wanted the pool to follow the natural line of the harbour,' says Kerridge. Alongside the pool is a hardwood canopy that filters the sunlight onto a deck below. As the kitchen is some distance from the pool area, Kerridge also included a built-in barbecue and preparation area. In contrast to the covered deck, a spa pool with a curved timber seat catches the full sun. Adjacent to the pool, the owners can sunbake or dip into the spa to cool off.

While the owners regularly travel, they are spending more of their time at home. 'They felt like they were staying in a resort as soon as they moved in,' says Kerridge.

PHOTOGRAPHY BY BRETT BOARDMAN

# A THERMAL ENVIRONMENT

## DE CAMPO ARCHITECTS

This house, designed by de Campo Architects, is one of two large townhouses. An Edwardian-style weatherboard house was demolished to make way for these new homes, which are each approximately 370 square metres in size. While insulated precast panels have been used extensively to create controlled thermal environments in wineries and cold storage areas, to the architect's knowledge, these panels are rarely used for domestic purposes.

The brief was to create a comfortable home with 'street appeal' and spacious living areas with strong connections to the outdoor spaces. The ground floor of the houses consists of the living area (adjacent to the terrace), a dining room and a kitchen. Each of the three areas is defined with a small change in floor level. On the subterranean level is the garage and office. And above the main living areas, on the third level are the bedrooms and bathrooms. From the living areas and the bedrooms above, there's a view of the pool, appearing to cantilever over the leafy street below.

The first glimpse of the pool is through a slot in the front fence. As you climb the steps to the main entrance, the presence of water intensifies. 'My clients wanted a pool that could be used for recreation as well being decorative'. The pool, approximately 5.5 metres in length and 2 metres wide, is relatively deep, at 2.5 metres. Directly below the shallow end of the pool, adjacent to the garage below, is the plant room. 'My clients have young children and they wanted to be able to use the pool for games, as well as for swimming laps,' says de Campo.

The walls in the house have also been staggered to increase the light entering the home and to offer different glimpses of the pool. As de Campo says, 'The water provides a contrast to the home's off-formed concrete'.

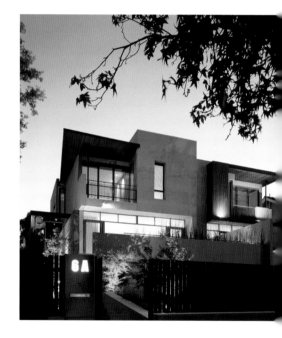

# THREE BODIES OF WATER

BBP ARCHITECTS

Once overgrown scrubland, this coastal property is now perfectly manicured with a pool and tennis court. 'The site was heavily covered. It was difficult to ascertain the exact topography of the land,' says architect David Balestra-Pimpini of BBP Architects, who designed the house with architect Serge Biguzas, co-director of the practice.

The house fans across the site in the form of two interlocking wings. One wing is for children and guests. The other wing includes the kitchen, dining and living areas. A substantial house of approximately 500 square metres, the brief to the architects included a garage to accommodate three cars and a boat.

Large cedar sliding doors surrounding the main living area blur the division between indoor and outdoor spaces. Frosted glass sliding doors, framing the second living area/parents' retreat, also relax the divisions within the home. 'There are elements from a traditional Japanese-style house. These walls can be pulled across to enclose the second living area completely,' says Balestra-Pimpini. 'It's important to be able to articulate different spaces,' he adds.

There are three bodies of water around this home, all carefully orchestrated. Like many Japanese homes, the use of water is integral to the design of the house. In the courtyard that intersects the two pavilions, is a waterbed of white marble stones. Framed in bluestone, water spills over the edge and creates a contemplative aspect from the kitchen and living areas. Outside the main bedroom is a plunge pool. Open to the sky, this area can be screened by timber-battened doors leading to the pool.

While this house is only a short walk to the beach, it doesn't have sea views. 'Our clients wanted to be reminded they were near the water. If they couldn't see the water, they certainly wanted to feel its presence,' says Balestra-Pimpini. 'There are days when our clients don't leave the house. And why should they have to. It's all here'.

PHOTOGRAPHY BY SHANIA SHEGEDYN

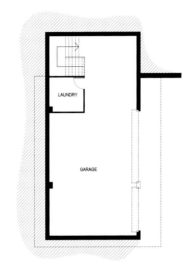

# TRANQUIL WATERS

## PERKINS ARCHITECTS

This house was designed for a couple with teenage children. They were leaving behind a large ornate Edwardian-style home for something more contemporary. Designed by architect Ian Perkins, the house has two 'faces'; a public one on the street, and a private one overlooking a side courtyard. 'One of the owners works from home. The front office is fairly open to the street. But you're only offered filtered views of the courtyard through the slatted fence,' says Perkins.

While the site is generous, one of the neighbouring views is less than inspiring. Perkins Architects responded by creating deep (1.4 metres high)

revered windows to the courtyard. As a consequence, the view along the main passage of the home is directed towards the 12-metre-long pond on the edge of the house. Only 450 centimetres wide, the pond provides an interesting vista from the windows, as well as from the elongated slotted window at the home's entrance.

There is also a strong connection to water in the pond outside the bathroom. The sunken bath is separated from the pond by a large glass picture window framed with ivy. As Perkins says, 'It's not just making visual connections to water. It's also about the pleasure of hearing the movement of water'.

PHOTOGRAPHY BY PAUL MUIR

# TWO-LEVEL POND

## PERKINS ARCHITECTS

This Victorian church was recently converted into a home and office. Renovated by Ian Perkins Architects, the original church was relatively intact. Featuring raked seating and stained glass windows on each side, it was an inspiring conversion. However, while the church was centred on the altar, the renovation focused on the side courtyards. The architects reconfigured the main assembly space to create two platforms as a result of the generous ceiling heights. The leadlight windows were reworked. 'We left the original stained glass windows. But we extended the windows to ground level to increase the light,'

says architect Ian Perkins. 'We wanted to make a visual connection to the courtyards'.

Glazed floor-to-ceiling walls separate the dining area from the main passage. And from this space, there's a view to the elevated pond in the courtyard. Constructed of bluestone and rendered brickwork, the pond was designed on two levels, with water flowing into the lower level. Large bluestone pavers and steps allow people to cross the pond. 'Elevating the pond creates a stronger connection to the interior spaces. The ledges around the pond also provide another place to sit,' says Perkins.

PHOTOGRAPHY BY PAUL MUIR

# WATER FOR COOLING

ENGELEN MOORE

Designed by Engelen Moore Architects, this inner-city Victorian terrace conceals a new glazed addition. A late 19th-century façade is presented to the street and to the rear is a contemporary lightweight informal living pavilion, facing a courtyard and laneway.

The lower level of the original rear wing was demolished and a new steel-framed structure was inserted to support the original upper level. This steel frame allows for the introduction of large glass sliding doors, a north-facing external deck with louvered roof above, and an 11-metre-long suspended steel pond. As there is a 2.5 metre slope (increasing towards the rear lane), the carport was located below the deck on the first level.

The pond, supported on a steel structure cantilevered from the side of the house, is 1.1 metres wide. Constructed of mild steel with an epoxy waterproof finish, the pond circulates filtered water via a pump. While the depth of the water is only 250 millimetres, it's an important component to the home's cooling system. Moisture from the water is drawn into the open plan living and kitchen area by gentle breezes. A glass door connected to the original part of the house allows cool air to circulate more freely.

Integral to the pond is a translucent glass screen wall, covering an existing brick fence to a neighbouring property. This glass screen extends to 1.5 metres above the top of the existing fence, allowing light to enter both this and the neighbouring property at different times of the day, while still maintaining privacy between the two. 'This area was simply leftover space. It was a place where bicycles were kept,' says architect Ian Moore. During the day, reflected light from the water bounces off the interior walls. And at night, the pond's underwater lights create a dramatic edge to the main living areas and the bedrooms on the level above. As Moore says, 'You're always conscious of the water. There's a soft gurgling sound as the water is recycled'.

PHOTOGRAPHY BY ROSS HONEYSETT

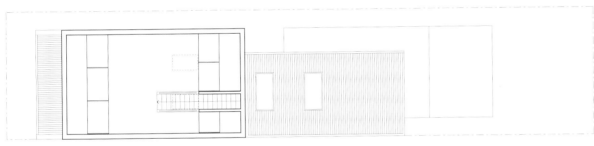

level 3

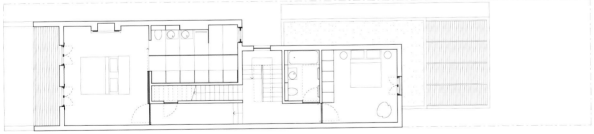

level 2

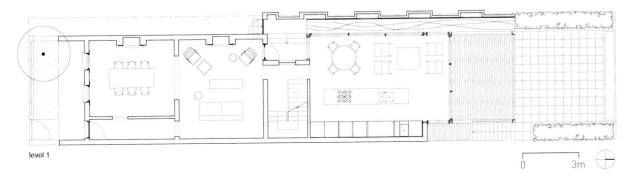

level 1

0     3m

# THE WATER HOUSE

DALE JONES-EVANS PTY LTD

This terrace is referred to as 'the water house'. Originally a two-level Victorian terrace, it has been transformed into four levels, including a new basement. The kitchen and living areas on the ground floor are surrounded by water. Designed by architect Dale Jones-Evans, the terrace features an internal pool lined with black river pebbles on the ground floor. Separating the living and dining areas at the front of the house from the kitchen and breakfast area to the rear, the dramatic pool is pivotal to the design.

A timber and steel staircase links the four levels in the house and appears to float above the watery mass (the staircase is suspended from the ceiling). Descending to the basement takes on an almost spiritual experience, as people appear to 'part the water'. Located below the light atrium, the movement of water creates whimsical shadows on the walls.

A pool in the back garden, also lined with black river pebbles, is magical. A small pavilion, hovering over the pool, provides an entirely new watery experience. 'It's like a grotto. Being black, you're not really aware of the depth or the distance of the pool,' says Jones-Evans. In the pavilion, a glass insertion has been made in the ceiling and the floorboards. Perfectly aligned, light streams through to the water below. 'The light is strongest at midday. It's like a shaft of light,' he says. To add movement to the water, the design of the pool includes one hundred strategically placed fine copper tubes. 'It's like an orchestra of water. There can be one hundred performers or perfect stillness'.

Rather than segmenting the water in the house, the pleasure comes from walking through and alongside the water. Fully integrated, the pool is a feature of all the living space. To reduce the division between the liquid and hard surfaces, Jones-Evans stained the timber on the treads and on the floorboards almost black. 'There's one large plane of space and the water is set flush to the floor level. The textures of the two mediums is the main division,' he says.

PHOTOGRAPHY BY PAUL GOSNEY, ASHLEY JONES-EVANS

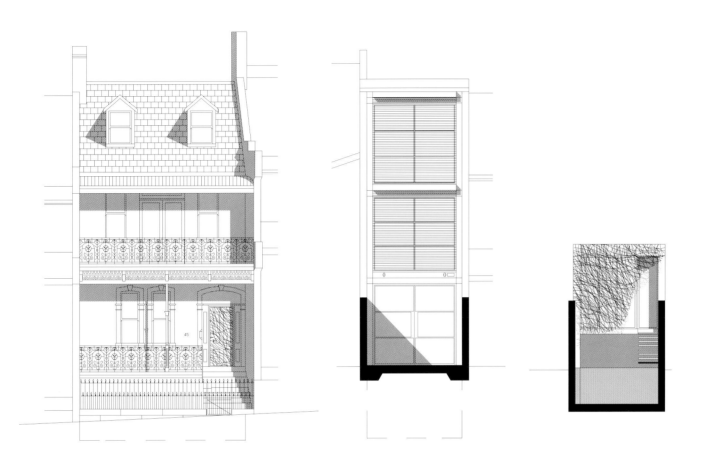

# WATER ILLUSIONS

## COY & YIONTIS ARCHITECTS

Past the front door of what was once a Victorian cottage, is a slick new home designed by Coy & Yiontis architects. Located on the edge of the city, this house takes the form of three 'pavilions'. The study and second bedroom at the front of the house form the first pavilion. The other two comprise the kitchen, living and dining on the ground level and the main bedroom and ensuite on the first level of the home.

Framing the central living space are two courtyards, one featuring a pond, the other a plunge pool. To reach the study, the owner walks outside and follows a covered walkway adjacent to the pond. 'The front pavilion is like a gatehouse. You experience the elements as you pass from one pavilion to the next,' says architect Rosa Coy. 'Our client works from home. It was important that he felt he was leaving the house and going to work,' she says.

The pond in the front courtyard is only 150 millimetres deep, while the plunge pool is two metres deep. However, the proportions of both pools (1.2 metres in width) together with glass walls on either side, creates the illusion that the pool runs under the main living area. 'Part of our client's brief was a plunge pool. We thought the pond would create a compositional tie in the design,' says Coy. 'The light also reflects from the water onto the living room ceiling and walls,' she adds.

As the house is relatively compact (180 square metres), the seemingly continuous band of water provides depth to the site. 'It appears to be one 18-metre-long lap pool,' says architect George Yiontis, who is seeing the move to smaller bodies of water. 'Not everyone has the space or is keen to maintain a large backyard pool,' he adds.

PHOTOGRAPHY BY PETER CLARKE

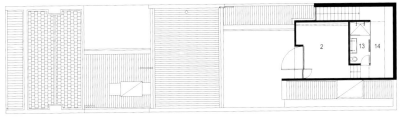

LEVEL 1

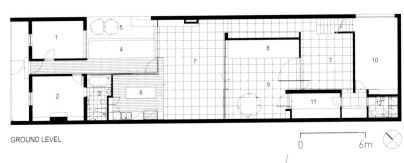

GROUND LEVEL

0 _____ 6m

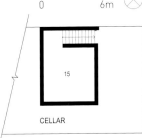

CELLAR

| | | | |
|---|---|---|---|
| 1 | Study | 9 | Terrace |
| 2 | Bedroom | 10 | Garage |
| 3 | Bathroom | 11 | Workshop |
| 4 | Pond | 12 | Laundry |
| 5 | Courtyard | 13 | Ensuite |
| 6 | Kitchen | 14 | Walk-in robe |
| 7 | Living room | 15 | Cellar |
| 8 | Pool | | |

# WATER SAVING SPACE

## INTERLANDI MANTESSO ARCHITECTS

There is little that remains of the original house, which was built approximately 20 years ago. 'The house wasn't particularly inviting. Most of the ceiling heights were 2.4 metres. In some places, the bulkheads reduced the height even further,' says Robert Ficarra, the project architect, who worked with Tony Interlandi. 'We tried to keep the original shell, but it just wasn't going to work,' says Ficarra. Apart from a high brick front fence that was remodelled, the only other feature retained in the new design was the garage. 'Our client is an avid art collector. He needed a gallery to hang the work. The existing walls wouldn't have done the work justice,' says Ficarra. 'He also wanted a more contemporary design'.

As the architects couldn't exceed the height of the original house, they used voids and three-dimensional spaces to accentuate the volume. The ground floor of the now 400-square-metre house contains the living and entertaining areas, together with a gallery. The bedrooms are located on the first floor. There is a view of the pool from the living areas and the main bedroom upstairs.

The swimming pool in the back garden was always there. However, the original design was considered too close to the building line, so the architects reduced the size of the pool by 1.5 metres, using the existing semicircular shape. 'It's still quite a generous-sized pool (approximately 10 metres in length),' says Ficarra.

In the front garden, concealed behind a high brick fence, the architects created a journey to the front door. A narrow channel of water was designed along one boundary. Approximately 400 millimetres wide and 10 metres long, the channel cuts a swathe through the front glass window and into the lobby. As Ficarra says, 'The landscaping is fairly minimal. The idea was to activate both the external and interior spaces with water. It creates a sense of harmony and directs your vision across the site'.

PHOTOGRAPHY BY GERRARD WARRENER

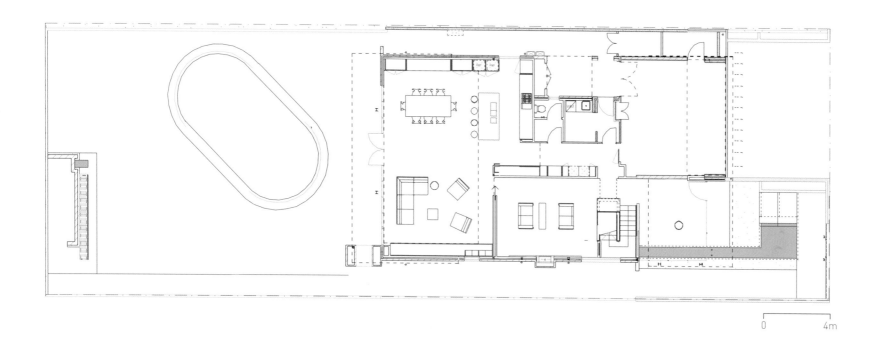

0　　　　4m

# A WATER WALL

## STEPHEN JOLSON ARCHITECT

This 1930's bungalow-style home was in its original condition when architect Stephen Jolson bought it for his own home. 'It was hardly touched, except for the pink render that had been added to the walls,' says Jolson, who fondly recalls the agent's remarks: 'Have a look through and I will meet you in the garden'.

Since then Jolson has extensively reworked the house. Walls have been removed and ceiling heights increased. A new kitchen, dining and lounge area were added to the original home and opened to the rear courtyard garden. Skylights have also been added to create light where areas were previously quite dark.

A new wing was also added to the original house. However, it is hidden from view from the main living areas. A glass-fronted pivotal door at the side of the living area conceals a passage leading to the main bedroom, ensuite and shower/spa area. 'The new wing is essentially a glass box,' says Jolson. On one side of the 'box', facing the living area is a rusted-steel laser-cut screen. This screen filters the light and acts as a veil for privacy.

On the other side of the bedroom, enjoying the morning sunlight is a 15-millimetre glass wall, splayed outwards. When it rains, water comes down the wall from the roof. When the conditions are dry, recycled water can be activated to create a constant flow. Jolson strategically placed lights in the garden, under the black bamboo. 'At night you feel like you're in a grotto. And during the day, the sunlight moves across the ceilings in unexpected ways. 'This room is about the movement of the sun' says Jolson.

A shower/spa, adjacent to the ensuite, looks directly into the tropical garden. A frameless 3-metre-high pivotal glass door in the spa allows access to the garden and views to the water wall.

While the inner-city house isn't large, measuring approximately 250 square metres, the site is relatively deep at 45 metres. It was that depth that first attracted Jolson to the property. As Jolson says, 'When you're reading in bed and looking out through the water, you could be anywhere. There's no sense of living in the inner city. It's an oasis'.

PHOTOGRAPHY BY MICK GUERIN

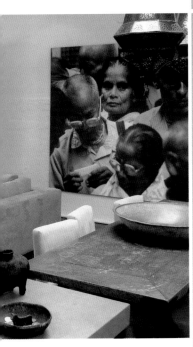

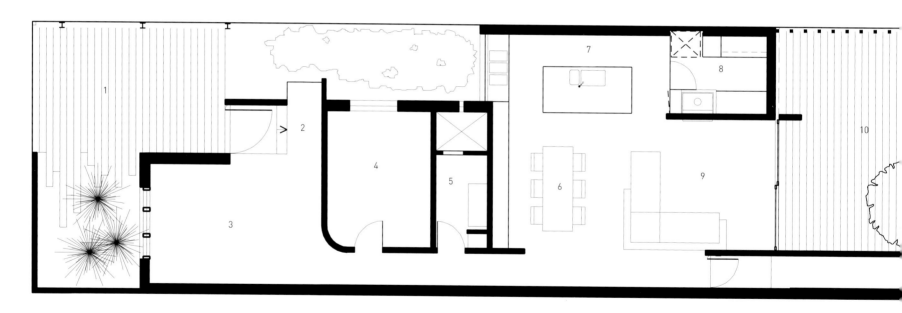

1  Carport
2  Entry
3  Home theatre
4  Bedroom 2
5  Bathroom
6  Dining
7  Kitchen
8  Laundry
9  Lounge
10 Courtyard
11 Master bedroom
12 Dressing
13 Master ensuite
14 Shower/spa

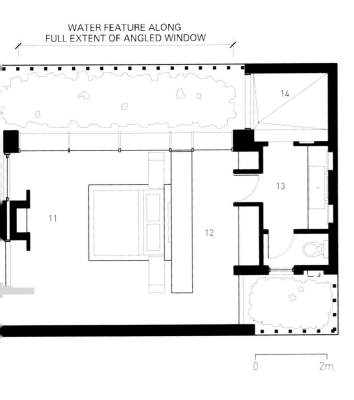

WATER FEATURE ALONG
FULL EXTENT OF ANGLED WINDOW

11

12

13

14

0        2m

# WATERY VIEWS

## DAVID PONTING ARCHITECTURE

This house, designed by architect David Ponting, is located in an historic area, close to the centre of town. With strict heritage controls, the architects were required to include a pitched roof, similar in form to the neighbouring homes. Keen to make a contemporary statement, Ponting elevated the pitched roof above the main structure of the house and inserted glass between the two. 'It looks as though it's floating,' says Ponting.

To ensure the house was at the same height as the neighbour's, the relatively narrow site was excavated by nearly 2 metres. This allowed for a third storey to be included in the design. The basement level contains car parking for four cars, a laundry and service room. The ground level was conceived as three distinct areas. One area consists of the family and living area, together with an office. The second area at ground level is the parents' retreat, accessed via an enclosed glass bridge. And the third area comprises the main bedroom and ensuite. On the upper level are the children's bedrooms and a mezzanine play area that overlooks the living area below.

The brief for the house was to be a 'sanctuary', even though it's only a five-minute drive from town. 'Our clients wanted something classical, yet still contemporary. They wanted a place they could escape to at the end of the day,' says Ponting, who separated the two glazed pavilions with a 33-metre lap pool. The lap pool flows beneath the glass floor of the bridge and to the edge of the main bedroom.

The pool is not only functional, but also offers watery views from within the interior. The main bedroom, for example, is perfectly aligned with the lap pool. At the end of the lap pool is a black glass mosaic tiled wall that channels water into the pool. 'At night this water feature is backlit. When the water trickles down this wall, it offers a sense of tranquillity, particularly from the main bedroom,' says Ponting.

PHOTOGRAPHY BY KALLAM MACLEOD

# A WET-EDGED POOL

STEPHEN JOLSON ARCHITECT

Made of rammed earth, this house gently cascades down its site. A protective shell for the home was created with four 5.5-metre blade walls, also made of rammed earth. Each blade wall relates to a module within the house and together they read as a weathered embankment in the landscape. 'These walls receive the harshest sunlight. The rammed earth is a blanket. It absorbs the heat and insulates the house,' says architect Stephen Jolson.

The owners of this home didn't rush out and commission an architect straight after they purchased this property. Instead, they lived in a rudimentary house (transported from a site nearby) for a couple of years and spent time familiarising themselves with every aspect of the site. While Jolson didn't spend as much time refining the design, he clearly embraced the property with the same affection.

In contrast to the rammed earth façade, the elevation towards the sea is completely glazed. From a separate guest wing at one end of the house to a study at the other, floor-to-ceiling glazed walls perfectly frame the view. The guest wing is another module, which is linked to the second module, the living and dining area, by an internal courtyard and 'link' (passage). The courtyard, planted with a 40-year-old olive tree, brings the owners and their guests together, even during inclement weather. 'There are strong winds down here. It was crucial to provide an enclosed external space,' says Jolson.

In contrast to the expansive living areas, the passage to the main bedroom, second bedroom and study is evocative of a laneway. Broad shallow steps gradually reduce in size. Light filters into the passage, particularly in the afternoon, accentuating the beauty of the rammed earth.

While the view towards the ocean is captivating, the wet-edged pool in the foreground is equally mesmerising. Set in a timber deck, the elevated concrete pool has a strong presence. 'My clients wanted a pool. But looking at it on paper with a pool fence didn't seem right,' says Jolson, who elevated the pool 1.2 metres eliminating the need for a fence. 'It appears like a simple box, void of any detail. The truth is it couldn't be any more detailed,' says Jolson, who concealed the plant room and pumps for the pool below the deck.

PHOTOGRAPHY BY SCOTT NEWETT

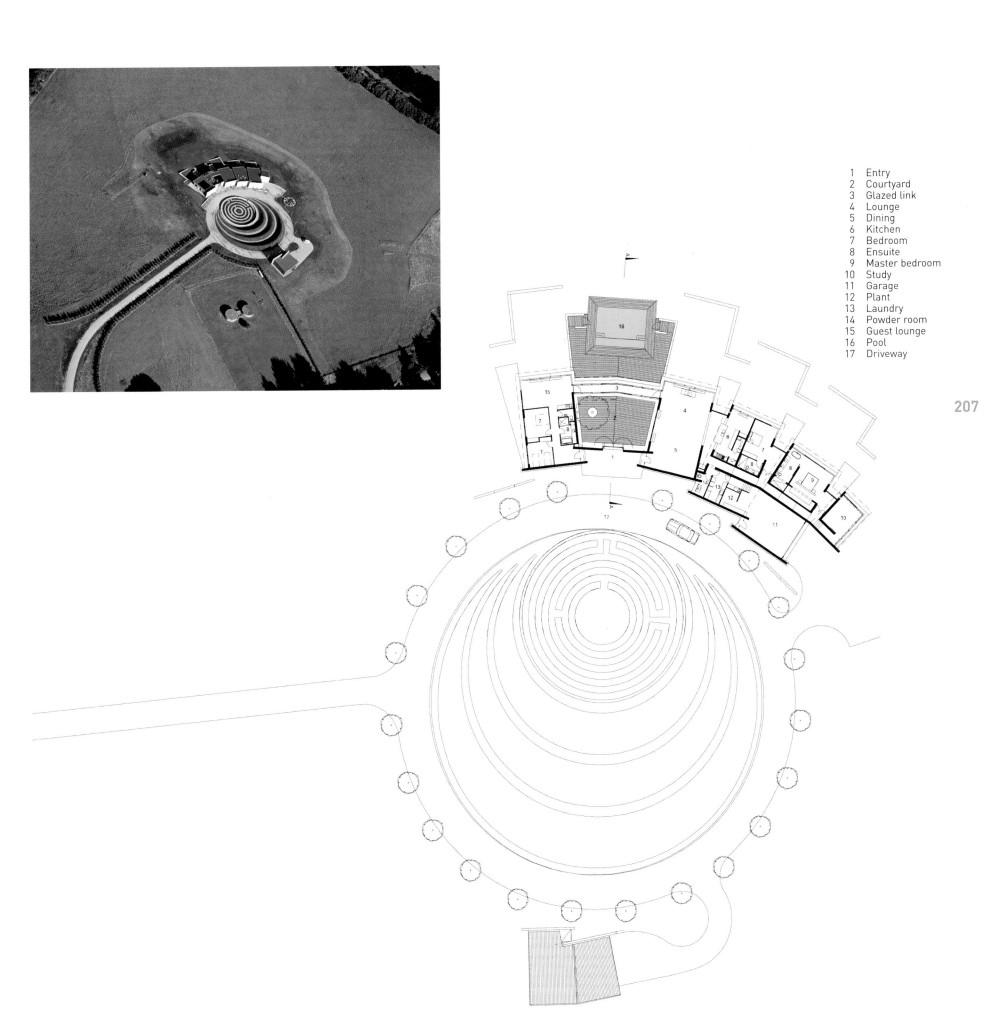

1 Entry
2 Courtyard
3 Glazed link
4 Lounge
5 Dining
6 Kitchen
7 Bedroom
8 Ensuite
9 Master bedroom
10 Study
11 Garage
12 Plant
13 Laundry
14 Powder room
15 Guest lounge
16 Pool
17 Driveway

207

# WRAPAROUND POOL

### , BUD BRANNIGAN ARCHITECT

This family home spreads across its site over three levels. 'We were restricted by the sloping site,' says Bud Branningan, who found it difficult to find the right position for the pool, a feature that was part of the owner's brief. 'It was a process of elimination. In the end, we decided to wrap the pool around the house,' he adds.

Constructed of plywood and cement render, the house features a garage on ground level, the kitchen and living areas on the middle level and bedrooms on the third level. The 6- by 3-metre pool shares three sides of the house and is visible from the kitchen and living areas, together with the stairwell that connects the three levels of the

home. Floor-to-ceiling glazing in the kitchen and living areas created an unimpeded view of the pool. Glass panels framing the staircase also offer glimpses of the pool. While the water and living areas are visually connected, access to the pool is via the kitchen door or alternatively through the laundry that leads to a terrace.

Brannigan was keen to create a sense of transparency in the house. Even from the rear terrace, one can see through the living areas and over the pool. As Brannigan says, 'I wanted the owners to be aware of the water all the time. The water isn't just a focal point in the house. It's used every second day'.

PHOTOGRAPHY BY DAVID SANDISON

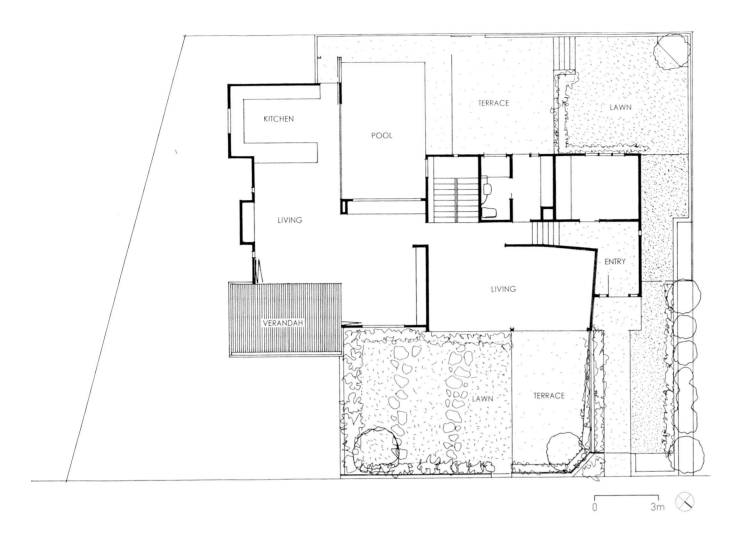

KITCHEN

POOL

TERRACE

LAWN

LIVING

VERANDAH

LIVING

ENTRY

LAWN

TERRACE

0   3m

# index of architects

# acknowledgments

I would like to thank all the architects featured in this book. Their designs, infused with water, are refreshing. Thanks must also go to the many photographers who contributed to making this book so special.

I would particularly like to thank my partner, Naomi, for her incredible support and constructive comments.

Stephen Crafti